DEALING
with the
CrazyMakers
in YOUR
LIFE

Dr. David Hawkins

HARVEST HOUSE PUBLISHERS

EUGENE, OREGON

Cover by Koechel Peterson & Associates, Inc., Minneapolis, Minnesota

This book contains stories in which the author has changed people's names and some details of their situations to protect their privacy.

DEALING WITH THE CRAZYMAKERS IN YOUR LIFE
Copyright © 2007 by David Hawkins
Published by Harvest House Publishers
Eugene, Oregon 97402

Hawkins, David 1951–
    Dealing with the crazymakers in your life / David Hawkins.
        p. cm.
    Includes bibliographical references.
    ISBN-13: 978-0-7369-1841-1 (pbk.)
    ISBN-10: 0-7369-1841-8 (pbk.)
    1. Interpersonal conflict—Religious aspects—Christianity. I. Title.
    BV4597.53.C58H39 2007
    158.2—dc22   2006024323

Printed in the United States of America

07 08 09 10 11 12 13 14 15 / LB-CF / 10 9 8 7 6 5 4 3

We may be tempted to use the term *crazy-makers* in jest. We might use it casually to describe anyone who upsets us. In reality, crazy-makers are neither funny nor fun. They are challenging at best and threatening at worst.

This book is dedicated to the countless clients who have shared their crazy-making stories with me during my 30-plus years of counseling. Many have struggled valiantly against people who have manipulatively twisted their words and emotions. I offer this book as a beacon of hope, offering insights and strategies for dealing with crazy-makers who use aggression to scare us, myriad hurts and wounds to make us feel sorry for them, and arrogance to overwhelm us. This book is written to help you set healthy boundaries and break free from such manipulation so you can be everything God intended for you to be.

Acknowledgments

Writing a book is a huge project, requiring a thoughtful and imaginative beginning, a nurtured and persistent middle, and a strong ending. It takes many contributors, and I am but one of them.

The inspiration for this book came in large part from my editor and friend, Terry Glaspey, as we sat having lunch at Maggies in Shelton, Washington. We joked about the crazy-makers we have known and spoke about the importance of writing a book like this. Thanks again, Terry, for believing in the importance of this project.

I am deeply indebted again to my wife, Christie, who joyfully read every chapter, offering keen insight and wisdom to improve my writing. I am blessed to have an in-home editor who asks—yes, asks!—to read my writing and offers powerful perceptions with grace. She knows how to deliver constructive criticism in a way that almost feels good. Thanks, Christie.

I have been blessed to have Jim Lemonds on my editorial team for another project. Jim, a trained and talented writer in his own right, always offers ways to strengthen the voice and flow of my writing. Thanks, Jim.

I have been blessed to again have Gene Skinner provide the copyediting of my book. We're a great team, man, and I so appreciate working with you.

Finally, I must again thank the team at Harvest House Publishers, who are more like a family to me every day. I won't try to name every one of them, but the number of godly professionals who work tirelessly to bring a book to print is incredible. As the number of books mount, and my relationships with these people grow, I count myself blessed to have them publishing and promoting my books.

Contents

PART ONE

Crazy-Making People

1

It's a Crazy-Making World

If despair comes to our own small lives,
so comes the avenue for allowing it
to deepen and change us.

CHRISTINA BALDWIN

Do you ever feel as if you're going crazy, wondering if the problem is with you or the people around you? Have you been in a conversation where your head starts swimming and you forget the topic of the conversation? Has someone close to you told you what you were feeling or perhaps even what you were thinking? Or have you been involved in a conversation, suddenly realizing you weren't following at all? Do you ever feel drawn into a conversation you didn't want to have in the first place?

For most of us, certain situations make us feel uncomfortable, and we wonder what is going on. Some people in our lives, often close family members, make us tense, on edge, irritable. Are we nuts? Are they nuts? Leaving our personal world, we've entered into the spinning world of the crazy-maker.

We all know crazy-makers, and even though we may feel ill-equipped to interact with them, we can develop some skills that will help us remain healthy while relating with them more effectively.

Just last week I saw three different people who were struggling with crazy-making people in their lives.

Sarah was first. She arrived noticeably agitated, fidgeting with the buttons on her blouse. She blurted, "I can't handle gardens with too much color. It's sensory overload. It reminds me of my family—random and out of control. I like gardens made of white flowers—they soothe me."

Sarah was 25 and single, taking drama classes at the local community college. She had come to see me for symptoms of depression. She appeared too thin for her modest frame, as if a strong wind might whisk her off her feet.

"Tell me more about your family," I said.

"They make me crazy," she said, waving her hands in the air. "I don't know why or even how. That's why I'm here. I've got to figure it out because they make me nuts, and I hate it."

"Be more specific, Sarah. Describe a family setting and what happens to you when you're in it."

"Okay, take this past weekend. First of all, it was chaotic. I stopped by to see my mom and stepdad. Everyone was talking at once. My sister was there too, and she always drives me nuts. My mom makes me feel crazy a minute after we're together, so the two of them at once feels like a zoo."

"What do they do to make you feel crazy?"

"My sister makes me feel crazy because everything has to be about her. She's a crisis queen. You know the kind—her life is always in an uproar. She's fighting with her boyfriend, who's a loser on drugs, and she wants to borrow more money from my parents. It's always about her. Heaven forbid that I have something going on in my life. She could never stand to give up the spotlight long enough for me to have any problems."

"What's her name?"

"My sister? Her name is Dena—but I call her Drama."

Sarah paused as though searching her files for additional evidence.

"Then there's my mom. She's on her fourth marriage. She can't seem to hang onto a man. She changes men like she changes outfits. And she does that a lot too, by the way. What she spends on clothes could feed a small country."

"What does she do that drives you crazy?"

"She and my sister always seem to compete to see who gets the most attention. Every time I share something, they've already been there, done that, and have the T-shirt."

"So what happened this past weekend?"

"Well, I wanted to talk about my drama class and my disappointment at not getting the part I wanted. Mom said Dena would have gotten the part and started talking about all the lead roles she played in high school. She did it to me again! Nothing I do is right or good enough. Mom never dreams big for me. Her life has been one disappointment after another, but she'd never admit it. I don't think she wants me to succeed. And it makes me mad."

"Parents ought to let their kids know it's okay to shoot for the stars."

Sarah shrugged her shoulders and laughed sardonically.

"What do you do if your parents can't dream big with you? Or what if they don't really listen to you or care how you feel about something disappointing in your life?"

"That's a shame," I said. "Parents who don't really listen to us cause us pain. We feel hurt and have to do some grieving as we get older. Sarah, you'll need to find a way to cheer yourself on if your parents can't."

"One of the crazy things is that I keep thinking she'll be able to cheer me on one of these days. But that day never comes. I always hope it will be different, but I end up leaving her house feeling disappointed. I feel punched in the gut every time I visit. Maybe I set myself up."

"Maybe so," I said. "Something inside all of us wants to be praised and encouraged by our parents. When they don't do it, we feel cheated. And we feel a little crazy."

A few hours later, I met with Becky. Though not related to Sarah, she could have been. Her story reflected similar problems with crazy-making.

Becky also suffered from depression, a common plight for those who were raised in or are now living in crazy-making environments. Although Becky had not grown up in a crazy-making home, she was living in a crazy-making marriage. She was a frazzled wife of 20 years and mother of two. She was 50 pounds overweight. Dressed in jeans and sweatshirt, she looked a good 10 years older than her 43 years. Her clothes were wrinkled and mismatched, as though she had picked out the first things she could find in the laundry basket.

"I'm a Christian," Becky had announced during one of her earlier sessions, "so I have to live with my choices. I don't really love my husband, but I can't change that. Who could love someone like him?"

"What do you mean?" I asked.

"Jeff's a perfectionist. He's about as much fun as a pencil salesman."

I smiled at Becky's comment.

"Becky, I'll assume that Jeff isn't really a pencil salesman. So what did you mean by your comment?"

"Jeff's about as colorless as a piece of typing paper. He's an engineer. He thinks like an engineer. I used to be an artist, but he's sucked that right out of me. I haven't created anything in years."

"How does he do that? Or how do you let him do that?"

"It's not hard. He criticizes everything I do. I share my dreams, and he shoots them down. I try to design something, working in my art studio, and he thinks I should get a full-time job. He says I'm dreaming. I think in possibilities. He gives me 20 reasons why my dream can't possibly come true. So guess what? After a while, I learned to keep my thoughts to myself—I feel like I'm going crazy."

"You must have loved Jeff at one time," I said.

"You know what? I don't really think I did. I think he was attracted to me when I was a wiry, dreamy college girl. I saw a practical man who would take care of me the rest of my life. And he's done an okay job of it, except for my emotional and spiritual growth."

"Tell me about your spiritual growth."

"Jeff is a Christian, but things are black-and-white for him. If I want to explore a new way to pray, he thinks I'm going New Age. If I want to explore different kinds of worship from what he's used to, he thinks I'm flipping out. It's his way or no way."

"And so you learned to shut down?" I asked.

"Yes, and it's killing me," Becky continued. "I can't do it anymore. I don't know what the answer is, but I can't keep living my life to please Jeff. It's just not working. It's driving me crazy."

"Why do you think it is getting to you now?" I asked.

"We have two teenage daughters, and I can't stand that they're growing up thinking that the life Jeff and I have is normal. It's not. I believe in keeping the family together for the kids and all, but this is nuts. I can't keep putting on an act for our girls. I want to teach them to live authentically, but I'm not sure how to do it."

"I have two sons of my own, Becky. I'd like them to see the world through their eyes, not just the way I see it. I can see that you want your daughters to be individuals."

"All I know," she said, "is that I can't live like this anymore."

"Maybe it's time to take back some of the power you've given away to Jeff. You seem to have given up your artistic pursuits because of him. Maybe it's time to regain some of your individuality."

"Of course you're right," she said firmly. "But standing up to his criticism is easier said than done."

The following day I met with Tim. At 15 he was filled with the usual angst one might expect to find in an adolescent. Tim, however, was not simply struggling with teenage issues of identity. Like Sarah and Becky, he was trying to deal with a crazy-making family.

Tim was the oldest of four children. His parents were very prominent in our community. His father was a highly respected doctor. Their home was in one of the nicest neighborhoods in our city, an area known as Pill Hill because of the number of physicians living there.

Tim's parents, John and Susan, brought him to see me several months ago after Tim had attempted suicide. Tim's aspirin overdose was not nearly lethal and was more embarrassing than anything to his parents. John was simply not going to permit mental health problems in his family. My marching orders were clear: Figure out why Tim would pull such a stunt.

Having told me point-blank that they expected Tim to snap out of it, I knew I had my work cut out for me, and I told them it wasn't going to be that simple.

I agreed to meet with Tim but made it clear that I would want to see the whole family fairly soon. The problem clearly went far beyond Tim's halfhearted attempt at an overdose. The problem was obviously the result of a dysfunctional family system.

Tim was incredibly bright. He had a quick, self-deprecating wit and refused to take his life or his family too seriously. He smirked when talking about how his father was the head of the local medical society and a member of several prestigious boards.

"Sometimes I feel like my dad wants me to call him Doctor just to confirm that he's really so mighty and important. He doesn't seem to understand that none of it means a thing to me. He's just a doctor. Not God."

Tim's anger oozed from him as soon as he plopped down in the chair in my office. He showed his disdain for his family's status in the community by wearing his long, brown hair pulled back in a ponytail, much to his parents' chagrin.

"So the suicide attempt…" I asked.

"It was nothing. Just me telling my parents I'm sick of living the way they expect me to live. Not going to do it anymore."

"Well, you sure got their attention," I said.

"I just want them to allow me to be me. That's all I want."

"And they won't let you?"

"Nope. They have a way of doing things, and that's the way it is. It's crazy. For example. My mom and dad belong to the elite church in town. Does that get them closer to God? My dad prays at all of our meals but never sits down and listens to what I think about God. He doesn't care about what I think. My mom gives in to whatever my dad wants—she says that's the way God wants it. I don't see that in the Bible. A lot of things about the way they live just don't fit me."

Tim was lanky and strong, yet he spurned athletics. He was friendly but not overly sociable. He found comfort in computers, and this too bothered his parents. His father had lettered in football at Yale and hoped his son would be athletically inclined as well. His father was a workaholic, and here too Tim was a disappointment. Grades and academic accomplishments meant little to him. Whatever his parents admired, Tim seemed to reject, and this caused incredible tension in their home.

While Tim's father made his mark in medicine, his mother made hers as a hypochondriac. The family's attention always seemed to be focused on his mother and her latest illness. Tim and his three siblings were raised primarily by the family nanny, whom Tim also resented.

Tim's antisocial difficulties seemed directly related to the family's dysfunction. His father's workaholic tendencies had created marital problems for years. No amount of his father's money could make his mother happy. She wanted love and affection, and these seemed impossible for his father to give her. She discovered the only way to get attention was to be ill.

Tim displayed an unusual amount of clarity about his family functioning.

"My mom is nuts," he said. "If she's not sick with one thing, she's sick with another. I haven't seen her leave our home, except for church on Sundays, more than a couple of times in the past two years. Dad goes to his board meetings and comes home late. I wouldn't be surprised if he's having an affair."

"Does that make you angry?" I asked.

"Maybe. Who wouldn't be mad about having a family like mine? Mom never spends time with us kids, and Dad's always working. I have a famous father, but who cares? It doesn't do us any good. We live in a big, fancy house and are expected to go to some Ivy League university. But the bottom line is that we know our parents don't really care about us."

Tim's anger was eating him alive, but all he could see was his parents' problems. He could recognize their issues very clearly but had little insight as to how they were affecting him. Neither parent took the time or energy to champion him or his siblings. He was reeling from blatant rejection—from his father's workaholism and his mother's desperate attempts to gain attention. His world was crazy.

Different People, Same Problem

Becky is nearly 20 years older than Sarah. They come from very different backgrounds yet have similar symptoms. Tim is just a teenager. He has his life ahead of him, yet he too struggles in a world that doesn't make sense. All three suffer from crazy-making environments: Tim, from parents who are rejecting and passively controlling; Becky, from a demanding husband; Sarah, from a crisis-oriented sister and scene-stealing mother. Consider how their crazy-making worlds impact Tim, Sarah, and Becky.

- All struggle with symptoms of depression.
- All have low self-esteem.
- All feel deprived and unappreciated.
- All feel crazy and helpless, especially when trying to assert themselves.
- All are desperate to change their lives.

Things seem clear from the outside looking in. Because we recognize the madness, we want to reach in and yell, "Stop it! This is crazy!" But it's not that simple. Tim, Sarah, and Becky are trapped in a web of confusion they don't fully understand or feel capable of controlling.

Do any of these scenarios sound familiar? Your life is obviously unique to you, but are you experiencing the effects of living in a crazy-making world?

Crazy-Makers

Tim, Sarah, and Becky have much to teach us. Each is enmeshed in a world of crazy-makers. None of them are truly living their own lives. Rather, their worlds are dictated, in large part, by people who have an inordinate amount of power to make them feel good or incredibly bad. People who manipulate their moods, their behaviors, and most importantly, their well-being.

A review of the lives of Tim, Sarah, and Becky reveals that all three have lost their identities. They are integrally involved with family members who are egocentric. In fact, this is a core factor of the crazy-making person—egocentricity. These people do not set out to manipulate and destroy another's world. Sadly, it comes naturally to them. They are rarely malicious—almost always they are acting out their own misery. Let's look a bit closer into their lives.

Sarah's sister and mother seek attention. This is one powerful form of crazy-making that we will talk about in more detail later in this book. We notice that Sarah calls her sister Drama, referring to her ability to instantly create chaos around her. This is one of the surest forms of crazy-making behaviors.

Becky was raised in a normal family yet fell victim to a crazy-making husband. She is married to a man who demands control, another sure sign of a crazy-maker. We see her world and identity continually shrinking as he tells her what to think and how to live. Her individuality gets lost in the process.

Finally, we witness Tim's mother, who is a hypochondriac. Her behavior shouts, "It's all about me and my illness!" Meanwhile, his father's workaholic lifestyle insists, "It's all about my busyness and my business." How does Tim stand a chance with parents who are so adept at wreaking havoc in their world?

We will explore many additional forms of crazy-making. But we won't stop there. Our goal is to examine solutions for taking power from the crazy-makers so that you can choose exactly how you will live.

No longer controlled by the crazy-makers, you will find a freedom you never knew existed.

Definitions of Crazy-Making

We owe a debt to Julia Cameron, renowned author of *The Artist's Way*, for helping identify crazy-makers in our lives. As an artist striving to let her artistic voice come alive, she was surprised to find so many people who not only refused to champion her true self as an artist but actually went out of their way to limit her growth. She helps us recognize the people in our lives who do just what the title *crazy-makers* suggests—they drive us crazy.

Cameron says crazy-makers create storm centers. Chaos. Drama. She says they create confusion and then pretend they want to help solve the problem. She says, "Crazy-makers are small on responsibility and big on blame."

I call them "energy suckers." You know the kind—when you are around them you feel like your very breath is being stolen from you.

My wife, Christie, and I have a friend (we'll call her Debbie) who qualifies as a drama queen. She is sociable, vibrant, and interesting. We like her—in small doses. The problem is that Debbie likes to talk about herself, and she views everything from her unique vantage point.

Even if I had just won the Nobel Prize for literature or if Christie were being solicited by the White House for design consultation, we wouldn't be able to get a word in edgewise because when Debbie talks, it's all about her.

This may sound humorous, but it can be exhausting. With only so much air to go around, sooner or later we start gasping. Christie and I look at one another, smiling and wondering if Debbie will ever stop to take a breath. When we realize that the energy is being sucked out of the room, the situation is no longer amusing.

Kaleel Jamison, author of *The Nibble Theory and the Kernel of Power*, has a similar theory to Cameron's. Jamison says "nibblers" always want to be in the big circle, and they will do anything to make yours a smaller circle. Nibblers bite at you to keep you in your place. They want to convey the message that they are big and you are small.

If you feel smaller than someone in your life, perhaps that person is nibbling away at your self-esteem.

Sometimes crazy-makers are not so benign. We don't smile when we are around them because we recognize they are militant and malicious. If a good feeling is in the room, they take it upon themselves to destroy it.

Drs. Rick Brinkman and Rick Kirchner write in their book *Dealing with People You Can't Stand* that these people are "snipers" who use "grenades" to damage those around them. Brinkman and Kirchner believe the snipers first identify your weaknesses and then use them against you. They may resort to put-downs behind your back or insult you directly in front of a crowd. All the while they smile, acting as if they are armed only with squirt guns. What harm could they really cause?

Egocentrism

Crazy-makers are, of course, not attacking us with squirt guns. Their weapons are loaded with lethal ammunition. Perhaps you are reading this book because someone in your life is using deadly force against you. Crazy-makers trumpet their innocence, but you know better. That swirl of dust around their feet didn't just appear out of nowhere—they created it. After reading this book, you will know even better how to disarm them and regain control of your life.

Crazy-makers are, above everything else, egocentric. They are frustrated with their lives, and as a result, they demand attention. Because they have not found a functional way to make their lives work, they become upset if they see your life going well. And if you have problems, they will readily zero in on them to further reduce your self-esteem. More than anything else, they want the world to revolve around them.

Aggressive people are angry at the world, hypochondriacs are extremely sad and lonely, and attention-seekers want to be surrounded by drama. All demand to be in the spotlight, and they are not willing to share it with anyone.

Most of us enjoy attention, but we understand that its usefulness is limited. Egocentrism creates a very small world. A world of one. It is a lonely and unhappy place.

As we examine how to deal with the immature, self-absorbed, egocentric crazy-makers, we will learn just how tiny and forlorn their world is. We will even learn to have compassion for them as we discover how to deal more effectively with them.

They Just Won't Listen

Perhaps you have attempted to get the crazy-maker in your life to change—with little success. Perhaps you have confronted her about her behavior—yet seen no change. Maybe you've demanded he sees a therapist—and been met with staunch refusal. Join the ranks of those caught in the maelstrom of the crazy-makers.

One of the most important things you will learn in this book is that crazy-makers often do not see what they are doing. For all of the destruction they perpetrate on others, they generally do not sit awake at night thinking of ways to make our lives more difficult. They are not reading books titled *The Crazy-Makers Guide to the Galaxy* or *How to Make Those You Love Lose Their Mind.*

They act this way without fully intending to harm anyone. Scott Peck, in his book *The Road Less Traveled,* does an excellent job of describing two different kinds of people. The first—most likely folks like you and me who read or write these kinds of books—tend to be overly responsible. We take responsibility not only for ourselves but often for others as well. The second group consists of those who are "under-responsible." They blame everyone else for their problems. Not only are they not responsible for your problems, they feel no responsibility for their own either. How crazy does that make you feel?

Crazy-makers have an uncanny way of escaping responsibility. They can dodge any bullet, all the while making you feel kind of nutty. *How did they do that?* you ask yourself after walking away feeling confused and ashamed. You thought for sure you had an airtight case, but they didn't hear a word of it. They didn't listen, and they certainly didn't absorb anything you had to say. This is because they are defensive—closed to any new information. They have a rigid way of viewing you and themselves, and that's the way it is.

Crazy-makers create trouble for everyone around them. They are long on problems and short on solutions. They draw you into their dilemmas and can make your head swim in a nanosecond. They pit people against each other and are extremely manipulative. This makes them dangerous—and that's why this book is about learning how to deal effectively with that danger.

No Cause for Surprise

In a world where people are often immature and shallow, lacking spiritual and emotional maturity, we shouldn't be surprised that crazy-makers have found a way to thrive. In fact, crazy-makers have been around forever. Listen to the words of the apostle Paul as he worked against the egocentric crazy-makers of his day:

> It is true that some preach Christ out of envy and rivalry, but others out of goodwill. The latter do so in love, knowing that I am put here for the defense of the gospel. The former preach Christ out of selfish ambition, not sincerely, supposing that they can stir up trouble for me while I am in chains (Philippians 1:15-17).

The apostle James differentiated between two kinds of wisdom. He pointed out that we will always have crazy-makers among us because their actions are "earthly" and may even be satanic.

> Who is wise and understanding among you? Let him show it by his good life, by deeds done in the humility that comes from wisdom. But if you harbor bitter envy and selfish ambition in your hearts, do not boast about it or deny the truth. Such "wisdom" does not come down from heaven but is earthly, unspiritual, of the devil. For where you have envy and selfish ambition, there you find disorder and every evil practice (James 3:14-16).

How often have you felt overwhelmed by people who were consumed by bitterness and envy? How about those who are enamored with selfish ambition? Both lack the capacity to live outside themselves long enough to honor others. It's truly all about them, and we know it.

A Way of Escape

Thankfully, we have a way to escape crazy-making—by following the way of Christ. Consider again the words of the apostle James:

> But the wisdom that comes from heaven is first of all pure; then peace-loving, considerate, submissive, full of mercy and good fruit, impartial and sincere. Peacemakers who sow in peace raise a harvest of righteousness (James 3:17).

We don't have to suffer along with crazy-makers. We don't have to get caught in their web of manipulation and deceit. There is a way to escape, and we will learn all about it in this book. We will explore the different lives of crazy-makers, what makes them tick, how we get hooked, and how to get unhooked.

If you have been manipulated by the manipulator—the one who uses manipulation to get what he wants—take heart. There is a pathway to freedom.

If you have been assaulted by the aggressor—the one who uses power and control to get you to conform to his wishes—take heart. You can regain control of your life. You can set boundaries that leave the blusterer blowing in the wind.

If you have been seduced by the sufferer—the one who can never seem to make her life work and wants you to fix her—take heart. You can learn to give back her problems and her responsibility for them. You can learn to establish healthier boundaries and set yourself free.

If you have been confounded by the camouflager—the one who disguises words and motives—take heart. You can learn how to avoid getting caught in her confusing words and mind games. You can learn to champion your own thinking, surrounding yourself with people who think and talk clearly.

In this book, you will learn about the tactics of the crazy-makers, and most importantly, you will learn how to take your life back. You will recognize what these crazy-makers are doing and what you can do in response. Ultimately, you can determine whether you'll need to end your relationship with the people who are driving you mad.

So join me as we create a plan to reclaim your freedom. It's your life, and you deserve to live it on your terms.

2

Broken
Chaos Detectors

In the middle of the journey of our life,
I came within a dark wood
where the straight way was lost.

Dante
The Divine Comedy

My wife and I recently returned from the Costa del Sol on the Mediterranean in Spain, where we luxuriated for two weeks. Each morning, we awakened to glorious sunshine bursting through our windows. We strolled the beaches and dined on terraces that overlooked the sea. We felt as if we were living in a fairy tale.

Owing to the good fortune of frequent-flier miles, we flew from Madrid to Seattle—by way of New York—in first class. It was our last bit of pampering before we returned to our normal lives.

Our stopover at JFK airport in New York was an unpleasant wake-up call. Babies screamed; businessmen rushed through the terminal, jabbering on their Blackberries; people jockeyed for position in lines; others sprawled on the floor, desperate for a few moments of sleep.

The scene—replete with teenagers in grubby jeans and torn T-shirts, businessmen dressed in power suits, and nouveau riche women bejeweled from head to toe—was simply too much to process. If the incredible din and the sardine-like cramming of flesh-on-flesh weren't enough to shake us, the odor of a metropolitan airport did the trick.

"I want to go back to Costa del Sol!" my wife exclaimed. "I can't take this!"

I couldn't have agreed more. Our chaos detectors blared their alarm:

Too much.
Can't take it.
Sensory overload.
Danger.
Get out now.

Dr. Fritz Perls, the father of Gestalt therapy, taught us that the mind strives to make sense out of things—even out of chaos. We seek to construct a whole from fragmented parts. It is one way to come to peace with life's disturbing elements. Another famous psychoanalyst, Viktor Frankl, said much the same thing—we need to make meaning of our lives.

That's what Tim was trying to do.

Tim's World

It's not easy for a 15-year-old to make sense of the world, especially a world as chaotic as Tim's. He watched his father leave the house at six each morning and arrive home at ten each evening. His mother slept much of the day.

Tim's father, John, believed that medicine was the only remaining honorable profession. His father and grandfather were doctors. Growing up, no one doubted that John would follow their prescribed path. He learned at a young age to deny his interests and pursue options that garnered his parents' approval.

John excelled in soccer and received a scholarship to Yale, where his father and grandfather had earned their degrees. He was an outstanding soccer player, and his excellence helped him gain recognition, which he desperately sought.

Although John loved architecture and design, he was raised in a family that talked only about patients, disease processes, and interventions. John had little conscious choice about his future profession. It would be medicine.

John graduated from Yale and then attended Johns Hopkins medical school. His academic prowess provided a steep trajectory into the adult working world. John became accustomed to working 16-hour days—10 to 12 at the office and another four to six making rounds at the hospital. The pace was fast and familiar. He wasn't satisfied just doing rounds—he performed them with excellence and perfection. He was oblivious to any chaos this caused his family.

Tim's mother, Susan, had worked as an RN prior to becoming a doctor's wife and having children. But John's job took center stage. She tried to deny her resentment; the only vestiges of it now were her stress-exacerbated health problems—arthritis, stomachaches, and other symptoms, possibly including fibromyalgia.

She learned early on that her husband was married to his work. Susan did not question the husband who controlled her and his family with a firm hand. He expected her to control the children the same way.

When I talked to Tim about his parents' marriage, the bitterness spilled out.

"What marriage? They don't really have a marriage. Mom stays with him because it's the 'Christian' thing to do. They don't have a relationship. I'm surprised they spent enough time together to have four children. Go figure."

"So your dad is dedicated to his work?" I asked.

"That's not the way I'd put it. I think they're both crazy. My mom had better run the house efficiently 'cuz my dad's like a drill sergeant who can't stand any chaos when he comes home. He can't see that he creates the chaos. He rushes into the house at night like Captain Von Trapp—you know, that guy in *The Sound of Music*. He whistles, and each of us has fifteen seconds to recite the day's events. Crazy! He wants an instant relationship, and that's not how things work."

"How do you feel when your dad pulls into the driveway?"

"I want to see him. I just wish he'd come home for dinner and spend real time with us. I wish he'd slow down. He comes into the house, and my mom becomes Superwife. I watch her rush to get the house picked up and heat up Dad's dinner."

"Do your parents seem to care for one another?"

"I've never seen them hug or anything. Like I told you, I'm surprised they have kids. My dad loves his work, and that's the only thing he loves. He wants to control Mom, and the one thing he can't control is her health. It drives him crazy."

I could see the pain in Tim's eyes as he talked about his family. His father was married to his work while his mother made sure the family was in order for his father. His mother finally became sick and tired of this make-believe family, and she expressed her feelings in her symptoms of poor health.

No wonder Tim was having trouble making sense of this world.

Sarah's History

Sarah, whose mother and sister seem to be addicted to chaos, shared more about her childhood during one of our many sessions. "It was always about my mom," she told me. "It was like she was addicted to the sound of her own voice. She could hear herself talking, but I sure don't think she heard me."

On a recent visit, her mother had greeted Sarah abruptly. "I'm glad you're here. You're not going to believe what happened to me today."

Sarah rolled her eyes. "She kept moving while she was talking. I had to follow her to have a conversation. I'd been there less than five minutes, and I already had a sinking feeling in my stomach. My mom was totally preoccupied with her crazy life and didn't have a breath to spare to ask about me."

"What did you do?" I asked.

"Kept following her around. It's what I always do."

"How were you feeling at this point?"

"That's when I started feeling depressed again. Hopeless. I wanted to run, but I'd just gotten there. I tried to get her attention, but it was useless."

"Then what happened?"

"I tried to interrupt her and tell her about my trip to California, to the wine country of Napa Valley. I thought she might be interested because she likes wines. She didn't miss a beat in her conversation and acted as if she didn't hear me.

"I had to wait half an hour for your aunt to meet me for lunch," Sarah said mockingly, referring to her mother. Sarah continued sharing her mother's comments.

"You know I don't have that kind of time to spare. And then I had to take back that dress I got for my birthday. Nothing fits right anymore."

"And it's been like that since you were a child?" I asked.

"Since the day I was born, my mom has been addicted to chaos. One man after another. One job after another. One house after another. I don't know if she plans it that way or if life just happens to her. I do know that she becomes sullen when she slows down. It's like she's trying to outrun her pain."

"Do you know whether there is a history of abuse in her background?" I said. "I wonder if she is depressed under the facade of all her busyness. Jumping from relationship to relationship, from marriage to marriage, from job to job—your mother must have issues she is trying desperately to avoid."

"I've spent my adult life wondering how my mom and sister can create so much chaos and still think it's normal."

"That's part of the deal, Sarah. They learn to operate as if it's a normal way of living. They become so addicted to the chaos—the adrenaline rush of it all—that it seems normal to them. The brain actually produces chemicals that give people a high from rushing around like that. They like to be the center of attention, and they demand that you fit yourself into their world. I'm sure I don't need to tell you that they're not going to fit themselves into yours."

"No chance of that."

"It's a good sign that their behavior doesn't seem normal to you.

If it did, you'd be addicted to chaos as well. But that doesn't seem to be the case. Didn't you say before that you like white flowers and peaceful things?"

"I grow flowers in my apartment—geraniums, pansies, some tulips. It's not much, but it soothes me. I sit there looking at the plants on my deck and write in my journal. A few poems. It's a great feeling. But I wish I could have a normal relationship with my mother."

"That would probably be difficult, at least at this point," I said. "Let's talk some more about your mom and see if we can come up with some new strategies that might help you from feeling crazy around her."

Becky's Story

Becky's history wasn't so much about chaos—she was not raised with it. Quite the opposite. She was raised to defer to men. Her father had been in the military and raised Becky and her sister to be submissive, to live in the shadow of a controlling man. She learned the importance of pleasing others, of putting her needs last. She learned that lesson well.

Conversely, her husband, Jeff, was raised by alcoholic parents who lived with constant chaos. His parents became angry when drinking, which became increasingly frequent. Becky told me that his parents were late-stage alcoholics who had whisky before dinner and several glasses of wine after dinner.

"They drink like crazy," Becky said. "We hate to go over there. They invite us for dinner, but they're half-crocked by the time we arrive. And they continually repeat the same stories about their lives when they were younger. I'm sick of them."

"They've been drinking like that ever since you've known Jeff?" I asked.

"As long as I've known him, they've been alcoholics."

"I know I don't like to even be around people who are drinking heavily. Tell me what it's like for you."

"I don't think it's just the alcohol. That's bad enough. But Jeff's dad has always been a womanizer. I wouldn't be surprised if his mother's had a few affairs too. That was their lifestyle. Jeff doesn't like to talk about it, but I know his parents hurt him a lot."

"It had to be a tough home to grow up in," I said.

"I feel sorry for Jeff. It's not fair for a kid to be raised in a situation like that. But he doesn't talk about it. Probably no surprise there."

"I suppose not."

"Sometimes I wonder if his life with them was like mine is with him," Becky said.

"I'm not sure I follow."

"I wonder if he learned not to think or feel. With his parents, I just stop talking. I stop thinking. I start planning my next grocery list so I don't have to listen to the story of their last cruise. I don't really care to hear about it again."

"And to think Jeff was raised with that," I said. "It doesn't excuse his behavior, but it makes you wonder how it affected him. No wonder he doesn't know how to share his feelings or ask about yours. It's no surprise that he likes to be in control, to overmanage his emotions, to overmanage your emotions. His world was pretty chaotic growing up. He probably doesn't have the slightest idea about emotions."

"That sure sounds like Jeff," Becky said softly. "He doesn't care to hear about any pain in my life—or about our kids' for that matter."

"Remind me about your kids," I said.

"Two daughters. Great girls, both living in town, going to college. I don't know how they've been affected by Jeff and me. Overall, they're doing pretty well. I haven't told them I'm going to counseling or that I am not sure about whether I want to stay with their father. I guess that's part of my craziness, huh?"

"Not necessarily," I said. "You have to decide how much of it is their business. Maybe a time will come when you'll want to tell them you're having some problems."

Becky remains in counseling, working on developing her identity separate from her husband. She has had a difficult time reawakening emotions she has learned to silence.

The Process of Addiction

We can easily wrap our brains around the notion of addiction to nicotine, alcohol, and drugs. We aren't as quick to comprehend addiction to chaos and the central role it plays in being a crazy-maker.

Sarah had a hard time understanding her mother's and sister's behavior.

"How can they race around like ants in an anthill?" she asked. "Why do they treat me like I don't exist? They look at me and talk to me, but they never hear what I say or care what I think."

"I don't think the key is that they don't care about what you say," I told her. "That may be too simplistic. But I think you're right when you say they never really hear what you have to say. They have an agenda that doesn't include you. It's truly all about them. Your sister and mother probably don't get along a whole lot better, but they may have a higher tolerance for chaos with one another."

"I don't get it," Sarah said with exasperation. "They matter to me. Why can't I matter to them?"

"Until you come to terms with it, you're going to feel mighty crazy around them."

"You're right. I *do* feel crazy around them. I want to grab them both by the neck, hold their faces in my hands, and scream, 'Hey, it's me, Sarah! I want you both to shut up just this once and listen to me!'"

"Do you think that would work?" I asked, smiling.

And with that, Sarah and I spent a great deal of time talking about addiction to chaos. We discussed how addiction can happen to anyone; Christians can become addicted just as surely as non-Christians.

What is addiction, other than becoming fully accustomed to a destructive process or substance? If we move blindly forward on one path long enough, we can believe it is the only path.

We talked about how her mother had, perhaps at an early age, started running from something inside herself. Sarah had heard stories from her aunt about how her mother was an unhappy girl, and then an unhappy young woman. Her mother discovered that frenetic activity could keep her from feeling unhappy. After she had run so fast for so long, running seemed to be the natural way of moving through her world. It would be too frightening to slow down, and she had no guide to help her do so.

Sarah wondered if her mother knew she was avoiding something by running so fast—by being addicted to chaos.

"I doubt it," I said, "not any more than alcoholics know that they began drinking excessively to avoid something painful in their lives. Pretty soon it's the tail wagging the dog, if you know what I mean. The alcoholic needs the alcohol, not for the delight of sipping the wine, but because the body craves the booze."

"So my mom doesn't know she is running without a purpose?"

"No, I don't think she has any awareness of it. She only knows she feels better flitting around from thing to thing, man to man, job to job. She starts to feel unhappy with something and puts that feeling aside by getting wild and crazy. Having a new man makes her happy, at least temporarily. Moving to a new town makes her happy for a short time. Getting a new home, decorating it—all these things give her a buzz."

"You're describing my mom to a T," Sarah said. "She's seems to be desperately looking for something to make her happy, never looking at herself as the source of her craziness. She has excuses for everything. Nothing is ever her responsibility."

"Maybe it's a little like telling alcoholics they're drinking too much," I said. "You keep thinking they're going to wise up and get it. But the addiction is too strong. It's the addiction that's driving them. In your mother's case, her addiction to chaos is her driving force."

The Power of Ego

Working with Sarah seemed a bit like walking with Dorothy through the land of Oz. In *The Wizard of Oz*, Dorothy leaves the frightening wizard, who stays comfortably in the castle he has created, the place from which he can intimidate people.

Accompanied by the scarecrow, the tin man, the lion, and her dog, Toto, she overcomes many obstacles on her journey. When she comes back to the egotistical wizard for her reward, he drifts off without her. The ego cannot take her to the home she longs for. She despairs until the good witch Glinda reveals that she doesn't need the ego anymore, only her own readiness. Through her travels in Oz and her personal growth, she learns she does not need to rely on the ego to save her. Christina Baldwin, in her book on journal writing, *Life's Companion*, explains:

> We all live in Oz, and the transformation Dorothy makes is the same transformation we are all trying to make...As the ego becomes the servant instead of the master, we are able to see our life stories differently: to interpret events in terms of their purpose and growth.[1]

Sarah was being controlled by her mother and her egotistical power. But who can criticize Sarah for trying to get her mother's attention and affirmation? We all want to be loved and appreciated. But in order to heal herself, Sarah would need to learn to let go of her expectations of her mother and find meaning within herself and from God. Anything less would relegate her to her mother's crazy-making world.

Baldwin explains her theory about the powers of the ego and the pain involved in coming to an awareness about those addicted to chaos and ego-power:

> The ego...perceives itself as the only real self...So, in the midst of everything else that's going on, you will find yourself grieving. Or the ego may throw last-ditch fears and obstacles in your way. But there's a trick of the mind to be noted in all this: If the ego is so sure it's the only self, then who is it yelling at? Who is it trying to control?[2]

Over the course of several months, Sarah began to see what was truly happening. She began to see that her mother was driven helplessly by her own ego and her own fears.

So much of our distress in life comes from the power of the ego—the masterful self, the Wizard of Oz. Since the beginnings of the science of psychology we have been warned about the power of the almighty ego. We have learned that it really means Easing God

Out. Who needs God when we can control our own destiny? This, of course, is futile thinking.

The Scriptures are replete with warnings about how the ego, or fleshly self, can destroy us. The apostle Paul says it well:

> Those who live according to the sinful nature have their minds set on what that nature desires; but those who live in accordance with the Spirit have their minds set on what the Spirit desires. The mind of the sinful man is death, but the mind controlled by the Spirit is life and peace (Romans 8:5-6).

These are powerful verses and tell us much about our nature and the path to freedom. Who has not felt controlled, compelled even, to do things that were self-destructive? This is because we are controlled by our sinful nature. Thankfully, we are free when we live according to our regenerated spiritual nature. Paul continues:

> You, however, are controlled not by the sinful nature but by the Spirit, if the Spirit of God lives in you...If Christ is in you, your body is dead because of sin, yet your spirit is alive because of righteousness. And if the Spirit of him who raised Jesus from the dead is living in you, he who raised Christ from the dead will also give life to your mortal bodies through his Spirit, who lives in you (Romans 8:9-11).

The Power of Denial

The ego relies heavily on denial to remain in control. Making healthy choices is hard when we deny important realities like these:

- the pain we are causing ourselves
- the pain we cause others
- the ramifications of our behavior
- our own feelings

- the feelings of others
- our ability to make healthier choices
- that our choices are faulty
- our culpability in the problem
- what we are seeing

I have written previously about my experience with work addiction. This was, in large part, an addiction to chaos. It began innocently enough. I wanted to have it all. I wanted to raise a family, succeed in my private practice as a therapist, and go back to school for my doctorate. None of these ventures were bad. What was clearly wrong was believing I could do them all simultaneously at the expense of my family.

Desperately wanting to accomplish all of these things, I became obsessed with them. I narrowed my focus and set out on a journey to attain all that my heart desired. My ego gained superiority over my life. The train picked up steam, reaching a frenetic pace—a chaotic fervor. When I entered school, I denied my exhaustion. I silenced any criticism from family and friends that said I was taking on too much (more denial). I didn't want to hear their messages.

At the same time, I wanted to succeed in private practice. This required investing inordinate amounts of time attending to the day-to-day running of the practice, accepting speaking engagements to promote the business, and catering to the requests of referral sources.

Most important, I wanted to be a good husband and father. These roles were important to me, but I falsely assumed that I could give my family my leftover energies and that everything would be fine—once my life slowed down. Of course, my life never did slow down, and I paid a dear price in the form of marital problems and emotional distance from my sons. Even as the ship was sinking, I told myself I was doing nothing wrong. The power of addiction to my chaos was that strong.

The process of tolerating chaos in our lives is, in part, a process of tolerating denial.

Harriet Lerner, in her book *The Dance of Deception,* says that many of us don't really want to know the truth. We want to be spared knowing what is really going on.

Lerner writes about the wife of a university professor who tells her that if her husband is having an affair, she doesn't want to know. A mother of a teenage daughter tells her that if her daughter is using drugs, she really doesn't want to know. The owner of a successful law practice doesn't want to know if her daughter has been sexually abused by an uncle. The wife of a businessman doesn't want to know if her brother is struggling with suicidal thoughts and feelings. Facing these challenging situations is difficult.

> No one wants to be tricked, manipulated or duped. But, we may feel, at a particular moment, that we can't handle a more direct confrontation with what we already suspect or know. We are unlikely to seek "more truth" if we feel unable to manage it, or if we are not confident that potentially painful information is ultimately empowering and could lead to productive problem solving, more informed decision-making, and a more solid self in relationships. We vary widely in the degree to which we are in touch with our competencies to manage painful facts, and our readiness and willingness to move toward them.[3]

Perhaps, like me, you want to dismiss what Lerner says. You may see yourself as someone who can identify and confront reality. You may see yourself as someone who can look straight into the eyes of reality and make necessary changes. Maybe yes, maybe no.

How do we explain Tim's father's behavior? Does this incredibly intelligent man have no inkling that his son is in deep distress, to the point of making a halfhearted suicide gesture? He is a renowned medical doctor, but he can't see that his son is acting out for attention.

Or Sarah's mother and sister. Can't they see how exasperated and depressed Sarah becomes when trying to get a word in edgewise? Don't they have any understanding of what it must be like to live in her world, filled with confusion and looking for an understanding ear?

What about Becky? Has she just now realized that her husband is controlling and that the life he wants for her is far different from the life she wants for herself? What has it been like to walk in her shoes through countless years of giving up her spirit, her true self? And what about her husband? Does he really think she is fine and that things will be bright and rosy in their home tomorrow morning?

Each of these questions points to the power of denial. As Lerner says, we differ in our ability to face and name reality.

> Our knowledge and interpretation of the truth is, at best, partial, subjective and incomplete. But we all have varying capacities for empathy, intuition, refection, autonomy, objectivity, integrity, maturity, clarity, and courage—all of which enhance our ability to detect deception and incongruity in ourselves and others.[4]

Incongruities

As I mentioned previously, we strive to make sense, a gestalt, out of our worlds, as soiled and troubled as they may be. Each of us has this task, though it is quite difficult for the crazy-maker. How can crazy-makers make peace with their incongruities—the inconsistencies of their lives? How can they say they want happiness and peace and yet create chaos wherever they go? How can they go around making others crazy while believing they have little to do with it or perhaps not even noticing it?

Part of the answer lies in the understanding of incongruities. Many people have an extremely high tolerance for incongruities—living life with many inconsistencies. Saying one thing but doing another. Espousing certain values yet living life without incorporating these values into their lives. Their lives may not add up in our eyes, but they have found a way to make sense of them. They trip themselves up at every corner, but because of denial and tolerance, that is okay with them. Incongruities may not feel inconsistent to them at all.

We look into their lives and wonder, *How can you treat your loved ones the way you do?* The answer: Crazy-makers live in harmony with their incongruities. Because of massive denial, they are able to disconnect cause from consequence. They've found a unique way to create a gestalt out of it all.

But the crazy-makers aren't the only ones who have a high tolerance for incongruity. We must remind ourselves that Sarah keeps going to her mother's house, expecting things will be different this time. We must remind ourselves that Becky tolerates her husband's control and denies any semblance of autonomy for reasons she must come to understand. Even Tim, though young, will need to carve out his own individuality in the face of adversity without succumbing to self-destructive tendencies of depression.

Lest we become too judgmental of these individuals, we do well to remember that we have blind spots. We too live with incongruities. I read recently that the correlation between Christians' values and actions was quite low. In other words, what we say we believe has little connection to what we do in life. We believe in environmental causes yet give little of our time or energies to them. We believe in easing world poverty yet donate little of our resources to end it. We believe in equality yet cling tenaciously to what we have worked hard to keep. Incongruities exist among all of us.

Avoidance of Pain

Another window through which to view chaos addiction—the home of the crazy-maker—is the avoidance of pain. Addiction is, after all, a powerful way to avoid those things that hurt us. In fact, that is the essence of addictions: to avoid feeling pain and to seek pleasure. It is a primary issue in our culture and the source of many problems.

Consider how addiction (including addiction to chaos) is a way to cling to emotions that feel good and to avoid those that do not. Let's look again into the life of Tim's father, John.

We learned that John was groomed to be a physician from the time he was a child. He learned how to obtain his parents' approval and how to avoid their disapproval. The worlds of athletics and academics gave him extraordinary power. At an early age, he became addicted to this power. He enjoyed this feeling of control and disdained the feelings associated with losing.

John's life continued to gain momentum. Like other addicts, he learned to resist certain feelings, such as fear and pain. Having deadened his emotions, he couldn't learn from them. He never allowed himself to feel sad or hurt. Even a hint of painful emotions drove him further and faster into the world where he wielded power and control.

John moved deftly into the world of medicine. He became a hardworking and successful surgeon. In the fast-paced world of medicine, he truly learned to wield power. He continued to live at a frenetic pace and soon accepted the adrenaline rush of his life as normal.

Stuck

Sarah, Tim, and Becky are stuck—in many ways, as much as their family members are stuck. They are caught in a vicious circle of destructive actions—being fixated on trying to change other people, only to have them resist their actions. I explored those behaviors and their consequences with each of them during therapy.

Sarah wanted to force her mother and sister to pay attention to her. She wanted her mother to slow down and actually listen to her. To want this so desperately and not get it was excruciating to her.

Tim wanted his parents' attention. He wanted his dad to come home and actually be a father to him. He wanted his mother to give up her concocted illnesses and return to being a loving mother.

Becky wanted her husband to change but had, for years, catered to his power. She saw him as the culprit for all her woes. The bottom line was that Becky needed to make healthy choices for herself. To choose to have her husband simply change would not be helpful, not only because she could not force change upon him but also because she needed to make adjustments of her own.

Wishful thinking is destined to fail. Sarah was not going to get her mother to let go of her addiction to chaos. Likewise, Tim's rebellion would never succeed at getting his parents to settle down and become a normal family. Becky's depression and passivity would not help her cope with her situation in the long run.

Sarah realized, at least at some level, that her sister and mother were going to continue being chaotic. She couldn't change that, which caused her a great deal of despair. She took their rejection personally, and this made her feel horrible. Tim drifted into feeling lost and lonely when thinking about his parents. He took their rejection personally and was overcome by hopelessness. When Becky interacted passively with her husband, she was bowing to his control.

Our work in the months ahead was to discuss how to expand their options, which would open up greater possibilities. They needed to learn how to do what Dorothy did in *The Wizard of Oz*—to make a spiritual shift.

We will talk more about this in the chapters that follow.

Numb

As chaos addicts rush about, denying their inner experiences and emotions, their world eventually becomes numb and numbing. Wielding power and manipulating others becomes second nature. They don't know how to live any other way. They become anesthetized to their inner world.

What must it be like to live numbly in a world where life is a blur? Where other people are a blur? Let's listen again to Becky talk about life with her controlling husband. She has learned, over many years, to deaden her pain.

"I learned to live according to my husband's expectations. Whatever I had to do so he would not be upset, I did. I learned to tiptoe around him. His intensity and control always scared me, and I never fully realized the toll they were taking on me until too late. That's when I came to therapy—after I had already become depressed. Now I'm learning how to listen to my feelings. I had to turn them off through most of my marriage just to survive. Even now it scares me to feel. What will I feel? Will I still want to save my marriage? In many ways, it was better not to know how unhappy I have been. It was safer there. It scares the daylights out of me to think and feel for myself."

Tim is learning—thankfully at a young age—to be honest about his feelings. Although he often expresses himself with anger and has been numb to many other feelings, he is finally starting to explore the origins of his pain.

"In my family, to talk about what I think has never been okay. Besides, who would care? My dad is gone, and my mom is sick. My family seems kind of dead to me."

Harriet Lerner talks about the importance of the family climate as it pertains to being able to speak the truth.

> The level of underground anxiety or emotional intensity in a family determines how much freedom individuals have to discover, clarify, and express their own truths—and how accurately they will see themselves and others. Anxieties drive people toward polarities, toward fusion or cut-off, toward glorifying or hating a difference, toward disclosing too much or too little, toward avoiding a subject entirely or focusing on it incessantly. Anxious families deny differences, sweeping them under the rug in a "group think" mentality that compromises individual autonomy, or they exaggerate differences and magnify them out of proportion.[5]

Lerner explains how people like Becky, Sarah, and Tim—and perhaps you—lose their voices and become numb. The process is insidious. It rarely happens in a short period of time but develops gradually over many years.

Tim's father could not abide anything negative happening in his home. The epitome of power and control, he wanted the perfect family. He wanted to come home to his wife, four kids, and dog Fido all living happily. He didn't want anything to be out of order. He was under incredible pressure and wanted nothing more than a few minutes to enjoy a warm fire and a glass of wine.

Sarah's mother had all the anxiety she could handle and more. She perpetuated her own calamities and led a crisis-filled life, so she had little energy for others. She lived as if she were kicking up a cloud of dust and couldn't see anything beyond her own nose. Her message to Sarah was clear: "Don't cause me any worries. I have enough of my own. Don't have any feelings because I don't have room for them, and I can't help you with them."

Becky learned not to create any problems. Her husband had control issues, and thus the family charter didn't allow for problems. Her husband's anxiety caused him to disallow any emotions that might make him feel uncomfortable.

Don't feel.

Don't hurt.

Don't talk about problems.

This is the definition of a crazy-making world because our emotional well-being actually hinges on our ability to talk about problems, share painful and joyful emotions, and state clearly what we are seeing. To learn to be numb is the beginning of craziness.

Coming Alive

A large part of the answer, for both the crazy-maker and for family members and friends, is to "come alive," to turn on our "chaos detectors" and recognize when we are numbing ourselves instead of sharing our feelings. This includes regaining the ability to speak and rename the truth. We cannot do this if we are numb and entrenched in denial or if we are firmly enmeshed in the crazy-maker's world. Healing begins with the smallest step of awareness.

Coming alive, however, is just the beginning. Reading this book will do you little good if you don't use it as a springboard for action. Consider the crazy-making relationship that you fall into again and again. You vow to do things differently but find yourself with the same feelings, the same expectations, and the same disappointments.

Consider some "two-degree changes" you can make, small steps you can link together to create real change. You can begin by journaling about the crazy-making relationship you have with a parent, sibling, or spouse. You can diagram what he or she says, how you react, and how you feel. These are very positive steps and set you moving in a different, far more constructive direction. Simply coming alive begins the process of change.

I close this chapter with inspirations from Henry David Thoreau, who clearly understood the importance of personal freedom:

> If one advances confidently in the direction of his dreams and endeavors to live the life which he has imagined, he will meet with a success unexpected in common hours.

3
They Come in All Kinds

Sell crazy someplace else.
We're all stocked up here.

MELVIN UDALL
As Good as It Gets

Not long ago, my wife invited friends from our business network group to our home for what she called "First Fridays." Christie loves to maintain friendships and meet new people, and she delights in entertaining. We agreed to have them over the first Friday of the month.

I watched as she made her lists—beverages, party favors, and finger foods. And then I watched her pore over the guest list.

"Do you think Jim and Terri will get along with the others?" she asked.

"Sure," I said, not really knowing if that was the truth.

"What about Nancy and Jenni?"

"I think they'll be great. Jenni may dominate the conversation at times, but she's always fun at a party."

"And how about Jake and Cathy?"

"Well," I said, "you know Jake is going to launch into a tirade about the Republicans and what a mess they're making of the Iraq

45

situation. That's what he does. People usually just nod their heads and go along with him. Except for Bill. If he shows up, there might be some political sparks. But we both know you can't control any of that. Just invite people and see who shows up."

"Okay," she said. "I guess we'll just see what happens."

The evening arrived, and nearly everyone on the invitation list showed up—married couples, singles, and one gay couple.

The consummate hostess, Christie was her usual gracious self. She greeted everyone with a big smile and told them she was happy they could make it. Soon our guests were eating, drinking, and mingling.

I cohosted and took notes.

I'll confess to being a little anxious about how the mix would work. I smiled and enjoyed myself. But this book and my interest in crazy-making caused me to survey the scene more closely and take note of the interactions. And sure enough, as the evening wore on, it became apparent that we had some crazy-makers in the group.

Let me provide you with a tour of the party and an introduction to our guests.

The Egotist

Dressed in a double-breasted Armani sports coat, hair coiffed, always on the lookout for a business deal, Jim was overly ingratiating—at first. He had the uncanny ability to offer a wonderful compliment to one of the other guess, immediately after which he launched into a conversation about himself. The sign of a true egotist.

"You look as beautiful as ever," I heard him say to Susan, a registered nurse. Susan politely asked Jim how he had been. He responded with a pitch that seemed very rehearsed.

"I'm working on a deal to buy that piece of property on the waterfront downtown—I'd like to build a motel and restaurant down there. I think I have a group of investors ready to go. I'm still looking for a few more if you know of anyone who might be interested." As always, he couldn't resist the chance to work a deal.

Susan asked whether the property could sustain that large of a project.

"Oh, that won't be a problem," Jim said. "I've got connections on the planning commission, and I know what it takes to get them on board. I probably don't have to tell you that what's important is *who* you know, not *what* you know. And believe me, I know the right people and understand how to work the system."

I listened for several more minutes as Jim shifted from Susan to others at the party. Each conversation turned out to be one-sided, with Jim talking exclusively about himself and his aspirations.

In spite of Jim's obvious egotism, I like him. He is fun, adventuresome, and most certainly full of himself. But I know I have to be careful around him lest I get caught up in a discussion about something I don't really care to talk about. I have to set firm boundaries, letting him know immediately that I'm not buying what he's selling. If I do that, and do it firmly, conversing with him can be enjoyable. When I falter, my eyes start circling in the back of my head, and I give Christie our secret, unspoken sign of distress, which means that she needs to come and rescue me.

Perhaps you know some egotists—the ones so full of themselves that they have little room for you. Having a balanced conversation with them is impossible. Talking with them can be entertaining, but at some point you begin to feel drained from listening to their larger-than-life accomplishments. In all of their talking, they forget something critically important—asking sincere questions about you. That's because you are not really an important part of their internal landscape unless they can profit in some way. They are big, you are small, and they drain your energy with insatiable demands. If you let them.

What is it like to be married to an egotist? They are so full of their ideas that their way of doing things has to be right. You have trouble getting your ideas and feelings validated. Life may be exciting because of the largeness of the egotist's life, but it can also be very tiring. They are right; you are wrong. They know everything; you are misinformed.

The egotist creates a strain on relationships and is one of our surest crazy-makers. Without warning, egotists will step forward and maximize their qualities while minimizing yours, making your head spin in the process. They make you feel crazy.

The Sufferer

Leaving Jim, I continued to greet people, stopping to listen to Katie, a gray-haired, moderately overweight woman in her fifties who appeared much older than her age.

"I can't seem to find a job that pays anything," she said to a small group that had gathered around her. "Living in Washington is nothing like it was in California. I could make twice as much there as here. And to top it off, I moved here to be close to my kids, but they don't seem to notice the sacrifices I've made. My daughter, Caroline, hasn't even invited me over for lunch yet, and I've been here six months. Not once. I don't know if it's Washingtonians or what, but people don't seem as friendly here as in California. All I do is go to work, come home, and eat in front of the TV. Nobody calls."

I watched and listened as Judy, another guest, fumbled with how to respond to Katie's complaints.

"Well, maybe you need to change jobs," Judy offered.

"I don't think that's an option," Katie said. "I work full-time just to pay the bills. I don't have the time or energy to look for other work. The doctor has me on medications to help with the depression, but I'm not sure they're working."

Judy fidgeted as she listened. She did her best to offer possible solutions to Katie's problems, but Katie immediately rejected each offer with a long explanation as to why it could never work.

Although Katie can be warm and friendly, her words always carry an undertone of negativism. She is stuck in a world of "poor me," where "nothing will ever work out." Like interacting with the egotist, talking at any length with the sufferer can be draining.

Katie is divorced. I don't know the reasons for her marital problems, but I can't help but wonder if she drained the life out of the relationship. Did she demand so much that her husband finally gave up trying to make her happy? Is she single now because no man can handle the burden of her never-ending problems?

Gary Chapman, in his book *Loving Solutions,* tells the story of a successful businessman who complains about his marriage.

> My problem is not with my business; it's with my wife. She seems unhappy and sad most of the time. I don't remember the last time I saw her smile. She is so negative and pessimistic about everything. She has been prophesying demise of the business for the last year and a half. She spends most mornings in bed, and in the afternoons she just sits around the house. She seems to have no ambition…To be truthful, life is pretty miserable at our house. I feel sorry for the kids, although they get more attention than I do. But, I know they wonder what is wrong with their mother.[1]

Welcome to the life of the sufferers. Although I'm sure they don't mean to be consumed by their problems, that is the case. Legitimately depressed people work at healing from their difficulties; sufferers seem to languish in personal unhappiness. The former group seeks opportunities, such as counseling and support groups, to recover from the painful situation; sufferers use the misery to gain attention.

The sufferer can suck the energy from a crowd of friends and family members in short order.

The Borderline

I continued to move around the room, greeting people, talking, laughing—and observing. Christie's eyes met mine, and we smiled. Both of us were enjoying the mix of people at our home. Different people, filled with life's joys and challenges. And as I was discovering, some of them filled with the ability to make life crazy for those around them.

Hearing Gail's voice, I meandered over to say hello to this attractive, 45-year old attorney. Dressed sharply in a dark blue skirt and bright yellow blouse, her long blond hair lay softly on her shoulders. Gail appeared confident as she interacted with two other guests and her husband, Dan. I took notes.

"My husband and I just got back from a wonderful trip to San

Francisco," Gail said. "We went to Sausalito again—you've got to visit that place. It was absolutely fabulous. But let me tell you about the people at the airline who treated us so badly," she continued. "We were supposed to have first-class tickets, and they had the gall to tell us the seats weren't available. I told them we had reserved them weeks before, but that didn't matter. Those people are idiots. They obviously didn't care about us. We took their names and told them we'd do our best to see that they lost their jobs. You can be sure that we'll *never* fly with them again."

"Didn't they even bother to apologize for the mistake?" a guest asked.

"Well, sure, they offered some feeble excuse," Gail said. "A lot of good that did us. What were we supposed to do? We didn't want to fly coach when we had reserved first-class."

"Were you compensated?"

"That's not the point. We had reserved first-class, and that's what we were supposed to have. We used to think the world of that airline, but no more. We're not going to be treated that way again. Right, Dan?" she said, looking to her husband.

Before he could answer Gail picked up where she had left off.

"I expect people to live up to their obligations. Dan doesn't care as much as he should about those things."

I glanced at Dan, curious about how he would react. His comments were telling.

"Honey, they gave us two free passes for our troubles and also gave us exit-row seats. I just think they were in a bind. They weren't intentionally trying to be rude," he said. "It wasn't that bad."

His words earned him a glare from his wife.

"Oh, it was that bad. Believe me. It was definitely that bad, no matter what kind of spin you try to put on it."

Welcome to the world of the borderline. Books have been written about her—known to be primarily a female disorder. Marriages have been destroyed by the moody volatility of those with borderline personality disorder. As I listened to Gail, I witnessed classical borderline tendencies:

- pervasive instability of moods
- difficulties with emotion regulation
- intense bouts of anger
- unstable social relationships
- shifting from idealizing someone to devaluing them
- sensitivity to rejection

Although I was not making a clinical diagnosis, I had seen Gail act this way before. Charming and delightful when things went her way, angry and acrimonious when they did not. Many people—including her husband—tiptoe around Gail. I watched Dan squirm in our presence and wondered what their relationship was like out of our view.

When talking about personalities, we should remember that not all borderlines are the same, any more than sufferers are all the same. In fact, clinician Christine Ann Lawson, in her book *Understanding the Borderline Mother,* identifies four types of borderline personality disorder.

- *The witch.* She unconsciously hates herself because she grew up in an environment that required complete submission to a hostile caregiver. The witch continues the cycle by acting cruelly to others. She feels little remorse for her hostility and harbors feelings of jealousy, betrayal, abandonment, and isolation.

- *The queen.* Queens want more attention, and they believe they deserve it. They feel a sense of entitlement, deprivation, anger, and frustration. They are intolerant and unable to handle frustration. Queens are capable of real manipulation to get the attention they so desperately crave.

- *The waif.* The waif feels worthless and desires to be loved and protected. Feeling helpless and hopeless, she masks her rage with sadness and depression. Although she looks to others to save her, she ultimately refuses others' help and mistrusts anyone who gets too close.

- *The hermit.* Hermits are terrified of not having control. They have a hard shell and are reluctant to let anyone get too close. Even family members experience "distrust, perfectionism, insecurity, anxiety, rage and paranoia."[2]

The Aggressor

I continued to mingle, happy in the knowledge that people were having a good time. I took particular interest in the variety of people, the differences in the personalities of those present. And then I began to imagine how each person acted in his or her marriage or primary relationship.

Suddenly, a commotion out on the deck caught my attention. I noticed Jake, the owner of a local auto parts store and an influential and successful businessman, talking heatedly to his wife, Cathy. I could see that he was intimidating her.

"I don't know why you had to say that," he said sharply. He stared at Cathy, one hand placed firmly on her shoulder. "I'm sick of you telling people things they have no business knowing."

"But I didn't say anything," Cathy said. She cowered under the intensity of Jake's words.

"Don't tell me what you said! I know what you said. Don't try to cop out of it."

I felt uneasy, watching this encounter. I noticed other guests noticing the commotion as well. All of a sudden the party stiffened. I sensed people being on edge, noticing but trying to continue with their conversations.

Just as people walk on eggshells around the female borderline, many do the same when around the aggressor, who is most often male.

Jake had a reputation as a hothead. I had seen him lose his temper before at our business meetings, once when he believed someone had spoken unkindly about him. His response was to publicly take this person to task. People seemed to walk softly around him. Jake could be quite demanding and self-centered as well. He often spearheaded political campaigns in town, and people knew to be careful around him. He could use his clout to make things difficult if you weren't careful. I now watched him use that same type of aggression against his wife.

When Jake noticed I had moved to Cathy's side, he quickly released his grip on his wife's shoulder. He smiled and motioned me outside.

"Hey, Doc. How are you? I've been meaning to talk to you." His tone was an obvious attempt to change the intensity and focus of the moment.

I looked over at Cathy. She was visibly shaking. I tried to be friendly as Jake talked to me about some changes he wanted to see made in our business network group. I felt manipulated and angry, though I tried to conceal my feelings. I struggled to decide if I should comment on his actions with his wife. As he talked, I kept an eye on Cathy, who by now had excused herself, presumably in an effort to escape from Jake and this humiliating situation.

I spoke with Jake for a few more minutes and then excused myself. His words came across as phony to me; he had clearly started the conversation simply to avoid the embarrassment of mistreating Cathy in public.

I walked into the kitchen, caught Christie's attention, and explained what had happened. Although there was little we could do, Christie shared my concern. We agreed she would seek out Cathy to see if she was all right.

Jake seemed to be the epitome of what Dr. Paul Meier, in his book *Don't Let the Jerks Get the Best of You,* calls "the jerk."

> The root cause of jerkiness is a sense of selfish "entitlement" that is both inborn and learned. "I deserve to act, be, or have what I want"...Jerks are more overt controllers who deliberately jerk people around because they enjoy the sense of power and control it gives them.[3]

Although I don't know Jake all that well, he certainly behaved like a jerk, both at our business meetings and now in our home. He had clearly attempted to intimidate his wife and manipulate me when I intervened. Let's look more closely at the conversation he had with Cathy and examine the effects of his crazy-making.

"I don't know why you had to say that."

Here, Jake scolds and intimidates his wife. He avoids sharing his feelings directly. He stares at her—another tool the aggressor uses to gain the upper hand and put the other person on the defensive. He places his hand on her shoulder, an unwanted invasion of her space and another method of gaining control. He has the audacity to act this way in public, which makes us wonder how he behaves in the privacy of their home.

"I'm sick of you telling people things they have no business knowing."

Now Jake tells his wife what she said, rather than sharing his concerns in a respectful way. Note that when she offers an explanation—a clear indicator she was feeling attacked—he doesn't accept it. His next words are preposterous.

"Don't tell me what you said! I know what you said. Don't try to cop out of it."

Jake acts incredibly "jerkish" and aggressive. He tells his wife what she said, a blatant violation of her boundaries. He further intimidates her by telling her not to "cop out of it." This is tantamount to him saying that she cannot think for herself and needs his help knowing how to behave.

Poor Cathy. I wondered what it was like for her to be in a relationship with someone who was so intimidating. What was it like to be married to a man who tried to control not only what you said but also how you said it? What was it like to be with someone who played mind-control games, trying to manipulate every conversation and situation?

The bottom line was that Jake seemed to have little regard for his wife's feelings.

A New Perspective

After the tense encounter with Jake, I stepped into my study for a respite. The party had lost a good measure of its buzz and joy.

Although I enjoyed attending the business network meetings, I was now looking at my colleagues through a new lens. I realized that crazy-making was all around me, even among those who were considered responsible, successful business people in my community.

I began to wonder whether I too was a crazy-maker at times.

I remember enjoying *Highlights* magazine for children. The section titled "Find the Hidden Objects" always fascinated me. Amazingly, right there in the middle of a picture of a farmhouse, complete with horse and barn, a dozen objects were totally hidden until I looked carefully and found them. When I did, I had an Aha! experience.

Why didn't I see that spoon before, I would wonder. *It was right there in plain sight. And there's the fork, leaning next to the fence in the tall grass in the field.*

The objects remained hidden until I looked at them with new eyes. Then they became obvious. I still appreciate the magazine and have found myself staring at a picture for ten minutes before some giggling seven-year-old client of mine points out the object I was unable to see.

Sitting in my study that evening, I had one of those Aha! moments. Crazy-makers can be a bit like hidden objects. You know they are out there. You know they are doing something that makes you feel kind of nutty. But you are unsure of exactly how they are doing it. And that is what makes your interactions with them particularly disorienting. That was how I began feeling at the party.

Identifying crazy-making behavior in others was one thing. But the next step was much more difficult: I began to reflect on how I have sometimes been controlling in my own life. I realized there are no distinct categories of "Jerk" and "Not Jerk," just as there is no clear delineation between "controlling" and "not controlling." But I was there, somewhere in the in-between.

I began to wonder, and worry, about my relationship with Christie. I pondered the following questions about my own aggressive and egotistical behavior:

- Had I ever used words to manipulate her thinking?
- Had I ever told her what she should say or think?

- Had I ever said or done anything to make her feel un-safe?
- Had I ever demanded my own way?

These questions haunted me as I considered Jake and Cathy's relationship. I know I can be overpowering in a verbal argument, and I realized I had sometimes used words to make Christie feel as though her thoughts and perspectives were not right. I now saw my behavior in a new light and felt ashamed. I vowed never to try to control anyone, especially Christie, in any way.

I also wondered about whether I exhibited behaviors associated with sufferers and borderlines.

- Do I ever wallow in self-pity for extra attention?
- Do I spend needless time worrying about problems rather than taking appropriate action to solve them?
- Do I ever act with shallow, righteous indignation when I have no right to that emotion?
- Do I manipulate people for my own benefit?

As I reflected on the questions, I decided the answer was sometimes yes and that I need to be careful of such actions. We are often put off by behaviors in others that we dislike in ourselves, and that was causing me some concern. I vowed that I will recognize these behaviors more quickly and strive to stop them.

Control

Was Jake and Cathy's argument merely an innocent spat? I don't think so. I heard what I heard and saw what I saw. Jake seemed over-powering. Cathy seemed threatened and frightened. She was crying, but he offered her no comfort. Rather, he seemed far more interested in looking good in my eyes.

Control is one of the favorite strategies of the aggressor, and it is a strong underlying characteristic of all crazy-makers. The borderline certainly uses control. The sufferer uses it passive-aggressively, and of course, it is a powerful tool of the egotist. It is such an important topic that I have devoted our next chapter to understanding the crazy-makers' need to control others.

Sadly, these people use control because they feel weak, helpless, and insecure. Often, we don't see their insecurity, but it is there. Jake would have no need to be overbearing if he felt a sense of peace and security.

During your interactions with the crazy-makers in your life, remember that they don't feel a sense of security. Otherwise, they would never resort to their tactics.

Haman

The Scriptures are replete with examples of all kinds of people—including some crazy-makers. The people of the Bible experience much of the same drama we experience in our lives today. With new eyes and fresh perspectives, we can read between the lines and imagine what life would have been like with some of these characters.

One such person was Haman, a high-ranking official in the court of the Persian king Ahasuerus, also known as Xerxes. Haman was an enemy of the Jews. The king did not know that Queen Esther was a Jew, as was her cousin Mordecai.

The drama heightens when everyone bows down and honors Haman except for Mordecai.

> When Haman saw that Mordecai would not kneel down or pay him honor, he was enraged. Yet having learned who Mordecai's people were, he scorned the idea of killing only Mordecai. Instead Haman looked for a way to destroy all Mordecai's people, the Jews, throughout the whole kingdom of Xerxes (Esther 3:5-6).

Clearly Haman had a lust for power and an intense pride—he would probably fit quite well in the categories of egotist and aggressor. We learn that Haman is on a diabolical mission:

> Then Haman said to King Xerxes, "There is a certain people dispersed and scattered among the peoples in all the provinces of your kingdom whose customs are different

from those of all the other people and who do not obey the king's laws; it is not in the king's best interest to tolerate them. If it pleases the king, let a decree be issued to destroy them, and I will put ten thousand talents of silver into the royal treasury for the men who carry out this business" (Esther 3:8-9).

What a slippery character—a card-carrying crazy-maker. Remember that crazy-makers stir up trouble and turmoil wherever they go. Haman is not working to further the best interests of the king! He is looking out for number one—himself. He is conniving, manipulative, deceptive, and power-hungry. But he was also apparently smooth enough to convince the king to take action. "Keep the money and do with the people as you please," Xerxes told him.

It just so happened, however, that as Haman was plotting to kill Queen Esther's people, the king could not sleep. He decided to spend some time reading, and what he selected was very appropriate—a historical document that told of the actions of Mordecai, who had saved the king's life. He was surprised to find out that Mordecai had not been properly thanked for his heroic actions and made plans to honor him.

This further infuriated the jealous and petty Haman. His power was beginning to unravel.

Shortly thereafter, at a dinner party with Queen Esther and Haman, King Xerxes asked the queen to petition him for whatever she desired. The queen revealed her heritage and asked that the Jews be saved from annihilation. "For I and my people have been sold for destruction and slaughter and annihilation."

The king asked, "Who is he? Where is the man who has dared do such a thing?"

Esther said, "The adversary and enemy is this vile Haman." The king was enraged when he discovered Haman's plot. He announced that the gallows that had been prepared for Mordecai would be used for Haman.

This is crazy-making at its finest! An arrogant man measured his self-worth by the power he had over others. He recognized his king as his superior, but his ego was not solid enough to accept anyone else as his equal—it was his mortal downfall.

The Deeper Questions

We may easily dislike Haman and vilify his manipulative qualities, but we should ask how much of Haman is in each one of us. We can condemn passive-aggressive personalities without questioning how often we too attempt to utilize indirect anger.

Do we have crazy-making qualities? Do we thirst for power and control in deceptive ways? Do we want revenge when feeling pushed aside or hurt? These are the tough questions we must face up to.

The heinous Hamans of the world are not the only ones who drive us crazy. We invite many people into our lives without realizing their darker sides. We all know people with qualities like Haman who are incredibly egotistical—so full of themselves that we disappear. The sufferers in our world are never satisfied. They could win the lottery and still complain about how much they had to pay in taxes. The aggressors push their weight around, causing us to quake in fear when we hear them approach. And finally, we tiptoe around the borderlines, never knowing if they are going to be our friends or our enemies. Will they be smiling and pleasant or sour and sniping?

As we move through this book on crazy-making, you will need to recognize crazy-makers. We must first identify them if we are to be capable of keeping them from disrupting our lives.

Keep in mind, however, that we must be mindful not to be so critical of others that we fail to recognize crazy-making qualities in our own hearts. We can begin by asking ourselves deeper questions about our own tendencies toward crazy-making.

4
Control Freaks

*Controllers not only fear separateness but also fear
being found out, that is, discovering that others do not
see them as they see themselves.*

PATRICIA EVANS

We sent our guests home and straightened the house. Plopping down on the couch, exhausted, Christie and I reviewed the evening.

"It was nice so many people showed up," Christie said.

"Everyone I talked to said they were glad they came," I added. "Although I find it hard to believe that Cathy was enjoying herself."

"Well, we can't control how people behave."

"On the positive side," I said mischievously, "I found a few people to include in the crazy-making book."

Tired but generally pleased with the evening, we lingered over the episode between Jake and Cathy. Had they gone home and continued their argument, with Jake taking the upper hand?

How had Dan and Gail fared after the party? Did Gail launch back into her tirade against the airlines? Did Dan continue to let her have the stage? Mostly we reflected about the issue of control.

Readying ourselves for bed, Christie stopped and looked at me.

"Speaking of characters for your book, I almost forgot to tell you about an encounter I had," Christie said with obvious frustration. "Do you remember Darla?"

"Describe her," I said.

"She's the one who works at the bank. Tall, with red hair. Dresses really nice, laughs loud."

"Oh sure. She dominates our meetings with her opinions. She seems to need to have her way about every tiny thing on our agenda. People get pretty frustrated with her. What happened?"

"She cornered me," Christie continued. "She came into the kitchen asking if she could help, but before I knew it she had taken over. Telling me where to put things, rearranging my trays, telling me how to run a party. Generally taking control. I wasn't strong enough to ask her to leave. I was hooked. I felt crazy. So where would she fit in your book?"

"That's a good question," I said. "Actually, we may just have come up with another category—the control freak."

"Well," Christie said, "she was certainly controlling with me. Controlled my time and attention without any regard for others at our house. Controlling my kitchen. I'm not sure I liked her very much."

I continued to reflect on Christie's encounter with Darla and the importance of control when talking about crazy-makers. Dr. Paul Meier and Dr. Robert Wise, in their book *Crazy Makers,* define crazy-makers this way:

> [They are] people who consistently irritate and confront without taking responsibility or recognizing their limitations. They do not feel the impact or hurt caused by their chaotic obstinate behavior. Crazy-maker behavior ranges from being argumentative to being destructive. Depending on their lack of empathy, crazy-makers move by degrees from being difficult to being narcissistic. Totally self-absorbed, narcissistic persons are marked by indifference and unconcern.[1]

Applying this definition to the egotist, the sufferer, the borderline, and the aggressor, the theme of control is unavoidable.

- Egotists take control by assuming everything should center around them.

- Sufferers take control by means of a twisted form of egotism—their problems are always bigger than anyone else's, and nothing you can possibly do will help.

- Borderlines demand control by acting out in a dramatic and volatile manner. You are either their best friend or their worst enemy, and you can never be sure when things will turn.

- Aggressors use intimidation, anger, and perhaps even threats to gain control. They are experts at twisting your words, changing the subject, and heating up the conversation, all of which can make you feel very uncomfortable.

Although I've provided a limited list of crazy-makers, understand that within each kind is an infinite variety. However, they all have some common characteristics—especially control. So let's add the control freak to our list.

Each of our crazy-makers, including the control freak, fits this definition. They probably don't understand the pain and confusion their incessant erratic and chaotic behavior causes. Each has the power to make you feel crazy—some in ways you can predict yet still fail to manage effectively, others in ways you could never have anticipated. And they invariably make you feel frustrated and off-balance.

It's All About Control

Every perpetrator in our circle of crazy-makers has significant problems—most of them related to control. Crazy-makers are absorbed with their own agendas. They end up being controlling, either because they need to be in rigid control of themselves—primarily because they lack the flexibility that daily life requires—or because they need to be in control of others. The issue of power dominates their lives.

Because of deficits in personality, crazy-makers *must* have control. Some more than others.

Crazy-makers are everywhere. You feel their control quite blatantly. You know not to cross the aggressor or the borderline, so you walk on eggshells when around them. You know egotists have an agenda. They have the future mapped out, and your ideas must mirror their agenda, or they are worthless. The sufferers' control is less obvious—in fact, you may understand you're being controlled only when you discover that the topic must always remain on them and their problems. Drs. Meier and Wise offer this description of self-centeredness:

> Self-absorbed people generally maintain clandestine plans, because they desire to conceal their weaknesses. On top of this their diminished sense of empathy keeps them from "feeling" how this duplicity affects other people. Rather than being relationally oriented, they are agenda driven.[2]

One of the most frequent criticisms I hear from people living with or around crazy-makers is, "It's all about them!" Try as my clients might, they end up dancing to the crazy-maker's tune. They'd like to carry on a reciprocal relationship, but they can't because of the crazy-maker's need to be in control. Power is the overarching theme.

The Control Freak

So the control freak joins the four other primary types of crazy-makers in their club. People nod their head in recognition when we refer to control freaks because all of us have them in our lives. But let's learn more about this character, understanding that control is a common variable of the other crazy-makers and the trait that drives us absolutely crazy.

Most of us have had to contend with control freaks at some time in our lives. Fueled by powerful but hidden anxiety, they have an almost insatiable need to control. You may not be aware that their demands stem from their futile attempt to manage their own inner angst. They feel fearful, anxious, and vulnerable. As a result of a deep-seated sense of helplessness, they grasp one of the few coping mechanisms they have for managing their anxiety. They become controllers.

Some time ago I worked with a couple who epitomized the aggressive control freak and the victimized sufferer, both of whom were working overtime to control their overwhelming anxiety. Both believed that their world was spinning out of control. Although this couple was stuck together like glue, they fought much of the time. Psychologists refer to this type of relationship as hostile-dependent. They can't live with each other, and they can't live without one another.

Timothy and Nancy met at the singles group in their church. Both were in their late forties and had come out of painful marriages and divorces. They were good-looking, successful, and bright. Timothy was an ophthalmologist, and Nancy was a successful Realtor. They had been dating for nearly two years when they sought my counseling services.

"Tell me why you're here," I began.

Timothy immediately launched into a tirade about Nancy's work hours.

"I have limited time to be with Nancy because of my schedule," Timothy stated. "I have a busy practice and want to see her when I have free time. But she refuses to set her schedule to coincide with my time off."

"Do you see what's happening here?" Nancy said. "Why do I have to be the one to rearrange my schedule? I've been doing that ever since we met. I've already modified my schedule to please him, and he wants more. I've let friends and clients slip away to please him, and I'm starting to get resentful."

"That's not a very Christian attitude," Timothy said. "If she really cared about us, she'd make time available. She can set her own schedule; mine is dictated by my patients. I don't always know when a medical emergency is going to happen. But she can schedule appointments. She just doesn't want to do it. Where's the commitment?"

Nancy fidgeted in her chair, sighed deeply, and began to tear up.

"I make adjustment after adjustment, and it's never enough. I'm not sure I can do this any longer."

"You're just stubborn and willful," Timothy said. "You can change anything you want to change. You just don't want to do it. I'm not going to invest anything more in this relationship if you can't make time for me."

"Just a minute," I said. "I'm a little unclear here. Timothy, why is it up to Nancy to adjust her schedule to fit yours? It seems to me that it should be a mutual process. You both need to take responsibility for finding time to be together, don't you?"

Timothy suddenly switched topics.

"You don't know her," he said. "It's not just this issue. She also fights with me about money, church, and any number of other things. If I don't do things her way, then I have to live with having her priorities shoved down my throat."

"Like what?" I asked.

"Well, she demands that we go to church on Wednesday night, when that's one of the nights I'm free. I want to see her that night, but she insists that we attend services."

"And there's no way to negotiate something that works for both of you?"

"Ask her," Timothy said sarcastically. "She's the prima donna. She's the one who has to have her own way."

"Do you always talk to her like this?" I asked.

"What way?"

"Your words are biting, and your entire approach is very controlling. You talk about her demanding her way, but it seems like you're backing her into a corner."

"I knew this would happen," Timothy said, rolling his eyes. "Nancy gets people to feel sorry for her, and you're falling for it just like everyone else. I get labeled 'the control freak,' but she's the one in control. Who's getting their way here? It sure isn't me."

My job was to help this couple, but my work was obviously cut out for me.

Vicious Circle of Control

Timothy had a lot at stake in prevailing against Nancy and me. I could sense his panic when he saw that being aggressive would not automatically enable him to seize control. The emotional stakes were high. He needed to "win" in order to quell the anxiety he felt. When he was able to get Nancy to go along with his game plan, he felt calm and happy. In fact, this was how he gained satisfaction. But when she erected any kind of boundary, his tension increased. I could certainly feel the escalation of emotion in our session, but it was completely outside his awareness.

My work was to help Timothy calm down while steering him away from his insistence on controlling Nancy. He needed to learn to speak from his vulnerable self instead of letting his anxiety control him. He was frightened—that was clear. His fear became the fuel that propelled him to try to control Nancy and her choices. The problem was this: The more his anxiety controlled him, the more he tried to control her. The more she became defensive and withdrew from him, the more his anxiety increased. He was caught in a cycle of destructive behavior that he had probably experienced most of his life: a sense of loss followed by anxiety, control, partner withdrawal, anxiety, control. And Timothy had absolutely no insight into this destructive process!

Control freaks are firmly in the grip of "repetition compulsion"—the tendency to do the same thing again and again. They repeat a destructive pattern even though it never works for them. Control freaks are engaged in a losing proposition. At some point, their partners finally become exasperated enough to blow up, shut up, or give up. In the process, they get caught in the crazy-maker's trap.

I continued to work with Timothy and Nancy, trying to help him see his pattern of becoming angry, anxious, agitated, and perhaps even threatening. His behavior caused Nancy to withdraw from him emotionally, leading him to feel discouraged and even depressed. He had little insight into this process and was very reluctant to give up his pattern. After all, being in control was his primary coping strategy. He let go of it very reluctantly.

Tactics of the Control Freak

During one of our sessions, Timothy and Nancy shared how they had met and told me that many aspects of their relationship were positive and exciting. Both enjoyed the arts, particularly theater. They were strong Christians and were active in the ministry for singles at their church. As Nancy said, "The good times are so good, but the bad times are so bad." This dichotomy sometimes masks the problems at the heart of a relationship.

As we worked on their power struggle, I sensed Nancy's despair. I watched as she became increasingly flustered and confused. The more she tried to have a voice, the more Timothy used a variety of tactics to overwhelm her, often with success. With Nancy's every attempt to regain equilibrium, Timothy had a counter tactic. Let's look more closely at the control freak's methods.

You're the problem. One of control freaks' most powerful tactics is to do everything they can to make you believe you are the problem. They don't need to change; you do. "If it wasn't for you, we'd have a perfect relationship," they say. "If you didn't think the way you do and act the way you do, things would be wonderful." Of course, if you have any vulnerability at all, any sense of self-doubt—and most of us do—you can fall prey to this powerful tactic.

Let's talk about this—NOT! Control freaks are often overly willing to talk. But when they do talk, the result is often a lecture or scolding. Make no mistake about it—this is not a discussion. This is not an open-minded sharing of opinions. It does not involve looking at issues from several angles. Control freaks have all the truth, and anyone who disagrees with them is wrong. In fact, they may even line up experts to side with them, adding to the credibility of their opinion. They may pull out a book, a quote, or a Scripture that supports their point of view. How do you argue against an authority, a powerful quote, or—heaven forbid—the Bible? In order to defend yourself from control freaks, you must first understand that their attempts at "conversation" are not intended to be a sharing of information or a free expression of points of view. Their strategy is coercive communication—one person attempting to change the mind of another.

Shame on you! A close cousin to coercive, manipulative communication is the use of shame. Shameful communication often starts with phrases like these:

- I can't believe you think…
- Do you mean to tell me you're going to…
- What? You actually think…
- Can't you see that…
- Are you crazy?
- Are you nuts?

If you have any sense of insecurity, any vulnerability at all, and again, most of us do, these shame-based words will find their projected target. The goal of these controlling behaviors is most certainly to manipulate you, but also to allay the anxiety of the control freak.

Black-and-white thinking. The control freak thinks in black-and-white and allows no shades of gray. You may consider a full array of options and possibilities, but control freaks focus on minute details and zero in on them. Because they see things in black-and-white, you may have trouble getting them to understand you. You may be using abstract reasoning with them while they are using concrete reasoning with you.

Intimidation. If control freaks feel as if they are losing their grip on you or the discussion, they will resort to other tactics. They may try to intimidate you by badgering you, threatening you, deriding you and your thoughts, or using outright intimidation. They may threaten to leave you, sabotage the business you have formed together, or employ some other ridiculous action. Again, the purpose of this is to force you to concede on some issue and help them feel more in control—which lessens their anxiety.

Diminishing. Control freaks must make you smaller in order for them to feel in control. They might call you "stupid," "fool," or other derogatory names in order to get you to doubt yourself. Control freaks don't want you to be who you really are—that is too threatening to them. You must be what they want you to be, so they need to diminish you in some way.

Anger and abuse. Control freaks have a temper and let you know it. Little things set them off; big things make them fume. They use their anger for one reason: because they can. These adult two-year-olds have temper tantrums when things do not go their way. In fact, they become angry over the smallest things, often for reasons they don't even understand.

Control freaks' anger quickly turns ugly. With a small dose of annoyance, combined with a rigid point of view, they can become intolerable. They push and push their perspective until you want to scream—or until you do scream. Incensed by even a dollop of rage, they become excessively critical, judgmental, and demanding. They harp on a subject until you want to crawl under a rock and hide. This is abusive!

Rewriting history. Control freaks have their own unique viewpoint on the world. They see things differently and twist things to fit their point of view. This tactic is particularly effective at making others crazy.

Jake, the aggressive businessman from the party scene in our previous chapter, used this tactic with his wife, Cathy. In a moment of anger, and feeling particularly threatened, he told Cathy what she had said and done. He put his own spin on the events and steered them in a direction that suited his purposes.

Patricia Evans, in her book *Controlling People,* says that manipulators use confabulation at times. That is, when unsure of themselves they may actually make up events to fit their needs.

> Confabulations seem like actual memory, seem to be the truth to the person who confabulates. Confabulations are so like actual memory that when a person confabulates a reason for, say, anger, he or she thinks that it actually is

the reason for the anger. No wonder physical and verbal abusers so often appear to be telling the truth when they explain away their hurtful behavior.[3]

Imagine for a moment how crazy-making it is to be with people who make up the "truth" to suit their needs. They "remember" things so that they will always be in a positive light, and you, of course, will be wrong. They aren't afraid to fabricate events or put creative spin on statements you made in order to establish their case. Rewriting history by using confabulation is a particularly potent tactic of the control freak.

Sweetness. Control freaks are not always mean-tempered jerks. If they were, you wouldn't be with them. At times, they can be very sweet. After they have gotten their way, when they have quelled their inner anxiety by getting you to go along with their game plan, they become Mr. Nice Guy. You get all the goodies that drew you to them in the first place. As long as you play their game and go along with their way of thinking, you'll get sunshine and roses. This can be very addictive. You can be tempted to accede to their demands in exchange for the benefits that come your way when you do.

Control Freaks in the Pulpit

Are there control freaks in the church? Most definitely.

Anywhere people are in positions of power, you will find a few who are control freaks. Do dominating pastors really know how controlling they are? Let's take a deep breath and tiptoe into this troubling arena.

Controlling people are very good at studying others and discovering their weaknesses. That's why we should not be surprised that pastors are in a prime position to exploit the vulnerabilities of their parishioners.

George Simon, in his book *In Sheep's Clothing,* lists five characteristics that covertly aggressive people will exploit. Knowing them could save you a lot of heartache if you worship in a church with a controlling pastor.

First, the controlling pastor exploits naiveté. Many parishioners would never think their pastor could be manipulative and controlling. How could this godly man standing in front of you, preaching the gospel, possibly be devious and scheming? Why would he seek control, adoration, and riches instead of promoting the kingdom of God? The Scriptures warn us about wicked people with dishonorable intentions.

The second trait controlling pastors exploit is other people's over-conscientiousness. Many parishioners set high standards for themselves, and controlling pastors can use this seemingly noble action. You have a desire to serve and to be self-sacrificing. You want to be a good Christian, but you're your striving toward godliness can actually be exploited by a controlling pastor.

I have heard that 10 percent of the congregation does 90 percent of the work around the church. Unfortunately, this 10 percent is also very vulnerable to being overused by the pastoral staff. These hard-working, super-spiritual few have set themselves up to be exploited.

The third exploitable trait is low self-confidence. Controlling pastors seek those who will follow their lead regardless of the circumstances. They want those who will defer to them in any situation without questioning their motives or actions. This is a particularly troubling combination.

Some years ago I belonged to a church with an overly zealous and power-hungry pastor. He was on a meteoric rise to spiritual stardom, and he offered me an opportunity to go along for the ride. I was invited to be part of an elite group of people whom he prized and apparently appreciated. What I did not see at the time was my own vulnerability—my own need to be liked and admired. In the process, this pastor exploited me and many others who were willing to give him the power he craved. The others and I were terribly hurt when he distanced himself from us once he no longer needed us. Teaching classes and serving on boards one day, we were dismissed from service the next. We discovered that we had been sought for what we could offer him rather than for who we were.

The fourth trait is over-intellectualization. This trait causes the victim of manipulation to focus on discerning why the controlling person would behave as he does, rather than accept the fact that he is overly controlling. The over-intellectualizer, according to Simon, thinks that by understanding the causes of the troublesome behavior, he might be able to change the behavior. Over-intellectualization causes people to excuse bad behavior because they think they understand the root causes.

The fifth trait is emotional dependency. Many Christians are particularly vulnerable because they strive to be submissive. The Christian who fears being abandoned or rejected may be vulnerable to exploitation.

We may be tempted to place pastors on a pedestal, seeking their approval rather than finding our approval from God. When emotionally or spiritually dependent, we lean too heavily upon pastors. Rather than seek an authentic relationship with Jesus, we seek a more superficial relationship with our pastor. We are approval addicts. We get caught up in trying to meet the standards of men—and that is a recipe for danger.

Sensing our need for approval, controlling pastors use flattery to get us to see their view of the world. Flattery can take many forms, including paying you special attention or placing you in a prestigious position in the church. In my case, my former pastor not only paid me special attention but also made me a confidant. I fell prey to this flattery by offering him more power than was appropriate.

Like other control freaks, controlling pastors can be dangerous to our well-being. They can demand that we see things their way, accept their viewpoints and obey them, and maintain loyalty and allegiance to them. Like other control freaks, controlling pastors will seek to isolate you from others who dissent from their point of view.

As I stated previously, crazy-makers are everywhere—even in church. But a little knowledge will help you disengage from these crazy-making controllers. Knowing what to look for in a crazy-making controller will help you regain your personality and become the person God intended you to be.

Do You Know Any Control Freaks?

Controlling people seem to be everywhere. They are certainly in some of our pulpits, in powerful positions in the workplace and government, and sadly, in our personal relationships. One of the primary purposes of this book is to help you recognize crazy-makers in your world so you can create new coping strategies for dealing with them. Keep an eye out for the following traits of control freaks:

- They control conversations and focus attention on themselves.
- They think in black-and-white, focusing on details rather than looking at the big picture.
- They must be right.
- They need to prove that you are wrong.
- They tell you what to think.
- They rewrite history, twisting things to meet their needs.
- They often control through the use of money.
- They often control friends and free time.
- They tend to be jealous.
- They tend to be rigid.

Gary Chapman, author of *Loving Solutions,* devotes an entire chapter to the controlling personality, which he describes as a "dominant personality."

> If someone disagrees with the dominating personality, that person is seen as an obstacle in reaching the goal. The dominant personality is always ready to argue and convince the opponent that he is wrong. If the dominant personality cannot convince the opponent, he or she will sometimes intimidate him—whatever is necessary to reach the goal. Dominant personalities are goal-oriented, not relationship-oriented. They get things done, but they often hurt people in the process. To them, that is simply the cost of reaching the objective.[4]

If you have been controlled by people—and you probably have—this list may remind you of how difficult relationships with them can be. You may recall how small you feel; how cornered, manipulated, and managed; how diminished they make you seem.

Controllers, for all their wonderful qualities, can drain the energy and love out of their relationships.

Coping Strategies

So, what strategies can we use to deal effectively with crazy-makers? Let's begin with the control freak.

First, understand that control freaks feel anxious—that is their primary motivation for exerting so much control. If you can talk to them about their anxiety, helping them to talk about the origins of their fears, they will often calm down.

Second, remind yourself that their behavior is not personal. It is not about you. They are simply trying to protect themselves. They have been compulsive for a long time, and this is not a product of your relationship.

Third, speak from your most vulnerable self and help them to do the same. Help them to speak in "I" language, asking specifically for what they need. Helping them get focused on the major things will help dilute the minor ones.

Fourth, practice letting them know that you hear and understand their needs. Reassure them that they are being heard—something that is very important to them. Practice using techniques such as paraphrasing to help them realize you are hearing them.

Fifth, stay calm. Controllers tend to be anxious, so if you're not careful you can become agitated and anxious with them. Try to be a calming influence, letting them know that together you will be able to solve the present problem.

Sixth, choose to give them some of the control, but maintain some control for yourself. Choose your battles. Let them have their way on some issues. Avoid power struggles where both of you lose.

Finally, make demands on them as well. Let them know that you have your boundaries and demand respect for them. Practice relating in such a way that you acknowledge their strong needs, but let them know you expect them to acknowledge and respect your needs as well.

Consider what Jesus might say to, and about, the control freak—and other crazy-makers. Jesus began His ministry with the Sermon on the Mount, where He taught, "Blessed are the poor in spirit, for theirs is the kingdom of heaven" (Matthew 5:3). Here Jesus tells us that no one can have spiritual wealth in and of themselves. All are dependent upon God alone for spiritual salvation and grace. Anxious striving for power, wealth, and happiness will not work—we must seek God for our comfort, strength, and courage.

You Control You

Undoubtedly you are reading this book on crazy-makers because you have one or more in your life. You are probably troubled by how confused and anxious they make you feel. All of that is about to change.

Although crazy-makers have powerful control issues, remind yourself that you are ultimately in charge of you. At times being in a relationship with one of the five different crazy-makers discussed in this book may seem overwhelming, but you must remember that you can become stronger and stronger, which will make you less and less susceptible to the manipulations of the crazy-maker.

Whether you are married to a control freak, work for an aggressor, are best friends with a sufferer, are the son or daughter of a borderline, or live next to an egotist, this book can empower you. If you understand these controlling personalities, you will then be able to set healthier boundaries that will help you resist their control.

Please remember that only you control you. Regardless of what others say, what others think, or what they may do to influence you, you have choices. You can become stronger, and by doing so, you will learn to relate with crazy-makers in a healthier way.

PART TWO

Caught in the Crazy-Maker's Net

5

The Big Hook:
Aggressors and Egotists

O, it is excellent
To have a giant's strength,
but it is tyrannous
To use it like a giant.

WILLIAM SHAKESPEARE
Measure for Measure

My friend Kenny is a superb fisherman. He lives, breathes, and eats fishing. He has all the latest fishing gear—but not the kind you purchase at chain stores. Kenny buys from a crotchety old man with a specialty shop and an unlisted phone number. The old man caters only to *serious* sportsmen.

Outfitted with his spendy gear, Kenny boards his deep-hulled, jet-powered Alumaweld, ready for a day on the Columbia River, home to some of the best salmon fishing in the country. He has spent the winter fine-tuning his gear. Now, in early spring, he is prepared. Kenny has also invested in the latest electronic gadgetry. He is confident about being able to navigate the Columbia bar, where the bones of dozens of ships lie.

With his electronic equipment, deep-hulled boat, and fancy

fishing gear, he is not only able to find the fish, he is able to hook them and bring them in. I know—each year, he brings me savory filets of salmon.

Kenny is determined. He is focused. He is the consummate fisherman. He will use whatever he needs, spend whatever he must, to catch the big fish.

In much the same way, crazy-makers use a variety of lures to gain your attention and pull you in. You already know that crazy-makers come in different varieties and use a wide range of mechanisms to hook you. Their motive is to ensnare you and to manipulate you into agreeing with their game plan.

We learned in the last chapter that many crazy-makers want one thing—control—and depending on their personality type and their abilities, they often get it.

An Eye on the Hook

As you meander through life, be aware that crazy-makers are out there with big, juicy hooks, ready to make you their latest catch. You know how easily you can get hooked by crazy-makers. You know how often you encounter a control freak, sufferer, or aggressor who is ready to drain the energy from you.

I am reminded of a client I worked with who came to see me because of his legal and emotional problems. Chuck didn't want to see me, and I was not all that keen on working with him. But seeing court-mandated clients is my job. That's often how crazy-makers enter our lives—by obligation. The stage was set.

I received the referral from state social workers. Chuck, a 30-year-old single dad, was employed as a saw filer at a local mill. The referral said he had struck his adolescent son several times out of anger. His son was subsequently removed from his care. Chuck was required to attend counseling and enter a drug and alcohol treatment program if he wanted a chance to have his son returned to his care. He was not happy about doing either.

I prepared myself for dealing with an angry man—and I was not disappointed. Chuck was not only angry, he was also a bona fide crazy-maker—an aggressor—with a dose of alcoholism thrown in. When I reviewed with him the reason for seeing me, his words shot out like shells from a cannon.

"This is a bunch of bull!" Chuck shouted. "They take my kid and make me pay for classes I can't afford. All the government wants is to get my money. I've never been to a shrink before, and I don't need to see one now. They're blowing this whole thing out of proportion."

How was I going to work with a man who was both angry and irrational?

Chuck was an expert at throwing out accusations, shifting the blame, and attacking others. Even though I'd just met him, I was immediately thrown into the enemy camp. He created chaos so fast that I found myself backpedaling in attempt to hold him at bay. What was I going to focus on? How was I going to interest Chuck in making changes that he obviously didn't want? I had my work cut out for me, both personally and professionally.

I could see the hook. Chuck's strategy was to blame everyone else. I knew that my job would be difficult. But do you think I could stay away from the bait—the lure to try to change his rigid mind-set?

No. I wanted to defend my position, to get him to see that I was just one of many caring professionals in white hats who were dedicated to helping him. I yanked on that bait right away, and he reeled me in like a tuna in a feeding frenzy.

Yes, I took the bait—hook, line, and sinker, as they say. And before I knew, it I was arguing with Chuck.

"What do you mean?" I said in response to his accusations. "The state doesn't want your money. They're trying to protect your child."

"I knew you'd be on their side," Chuck said sarcastically. "You're bought and paid for. You read the report. You know they didn't need to take my kid. I slapped him because he mouthed off to me. Tell me you wouldn't do the same thing."

"I wouldn't do the same thing, Chuck," I said, trying hard to control my temper. "There are better ways to discipline kids than by slapping them."

"He was mouthing off to me," Chuck said. "I barely touched him. What I did was just enough to get his attention."

"Really?" I said. "That's not what I saw when I looked at some pictures. You left bruises on his face."

"Those pictures make it look a lot worse than it was."

Our conversation was going nowhere. I was getting more frustrated by the second. Chuck had me dancing—flailing *on* the hook, rather than avoiding it.

I had seen the hook. I had prepared for the hook. But skilled crazy-makers can reel in the best of us.

Have you ever felt as if you took the bait even after you saw it coming? One of the objectives of this book is to change that. We're going to learn specific strategies that will help us avoid getting hooked. We're going to become aware of how different types of crazy-makers use a variety of lures to hook us. With practice and knowledge, we can resist those lures and maintain our sanity.

Getting Hooked by the Aggressor

Possibly the least liked in our choir of five crazy-makers, the aggressor has the distinction of using anger as a primary weapon. Remember the schoolyard bully? The aggressor is the bully who never grew up. Aggressors are most likely to intimidate, threaten, and throw temper tantrums to get you to go along with their schemes. Albert Bernstein, in his delightful book *Emotional Vampires*, offers this explanation:

> There are few experiences more emotionally draining than being yelled at. If you've met a vampire Bully, you know. Like the rest of the Antisocial types, Bullies are hooked on excitement. Rage transports them into a simple and bloody alternate reality in which only the strong survive. In their own minds, they are the strong. In reality, their anger may be the source of their strength, but it's also their greatest weakness. Vampire Bullies like power, but they don't understand it...Bullies are more in touch

with their animal nature than most people. They use their primitive power to manipulate the animal in you.[1]

Is that how I got hooked? Was Chuck using his vampire bully to get the upper hand with me? Bernstein says bullies, or aggressors, use the primitive part of their brains more than the rest of us. Chuck was using his aggression to instill fear in me. But there's more. When your eyes start to circle in the back of your head and you can't put together a coherent thought, there's a reason.

> Bully hypnosis is crude, but effective. Bullies just attack and let your own nervous system do the rest. A Bully assault can bypass the rational part of your brain and set you down in a prehistoric alternate reality where there are only three choices: fight back, run away, or stand still and be eaten. It's the perfect bind; no matter which one you choose, you lose. The newer, smarter parts of your brain may realize what's happening, but they're so awash in chemicals and primitive impulses that they can do nothing but watch in horror as the grim drama unfolds.[2]

I was partially paralyzed in my encounter with Chuck—a common reaction to the bully is to be frozen. We can see what is happening, but because we are afraid, we are not able to utilize our mature faculties to counter the attack. We are hypnotized by the aggressor's brutish actions. Aggressors may not have to do much to maintain control except to snarl occasionally. They have discovered that anger brings them power. Once people cower in the face of their power or sink to the aggressor's level, the whole cycle is reinforced. They are able to remain angry and use it to their advantage—because they can.

Flinging Back the Hook

I jousted with Chuck, even as I felt the hook sink deeper into my flesh. Trapped by circumstances of his own making, Chuck refused to take responsibility for his actions. The result was a hostile, vindictive man who enjoyed backing other people into corners. I was his target, and he didn't hesitate to tell me that I was part of the group that had stolen his son. The feel-good psychologist in me wanted to change his mind; the human in me was paralyzed by fear and wanted to turn and run; the macho-man in me wanted to fight.

Part of me definitely wanted to let him have it. But that reaction would only plant the hook deeper because by doing so, I would be playing the game on his terms. I wanted to hand him back the hook. But how? Here were my choices:

Ignore the hook. Your mother may have told you that if you ignore bullies they will go away. Sadly, this rarely works. Bullies are already privy to these weak tactics and are seldom daunted. We are also often forced to interact with these people because of our job, our lifestyle, or our marriage. Like it or not, they are a part of our lives. Walking away may not always be an option, but if it is, consider it.

Notice the hook. We cannot help but be snagged by something that has sharp barbs. The Scriptures implore us to be watchful of dangers, or we are more likely to fall into temptation. We must keep our eyes open and be aware of these hooks.

Being mindful of this crazy-making process is a powerful antidote to getting hooked. Did Chuck's actions remind you of frightening times in your life? Bullies often trigger latent reactions, perhaps as far back as the schoolyard, when we were taunted and teased. Reminding ourselves that was then and this is now is a critical first step.

Watch the hook. Clearly, noticing the hook is not enough. It was not enough for me, and I'm a trained professional! Even seeing Chuck's blatantly aggressive stance did not stop me from biting down hard, swallowing, and then flailing about like a snared trout. He was in control, and I hated it.

We must not only notice the hook but watch what the fisherman does with it. Manipulation of the hook is what separates novice aggressors from the experts—and crazy-makers like Chuck are experts! They are like the bullies of childhood who taunt you, poke at you, say mean things, and prod you until you are ready to lash out at them.

Let the hook float by. The most effective way to deal with a bully is not to duke it out on the playground. Victory is gained in the battleground of the mind. This is where you can win the war. Stay in your logical brain, breathe, and detach from the primitive reaction that wants to spit, kick, and call names. Stay in control of the situation. Notice how angry you are. Recognize that you would like to lash out. These are all tools that will allow you to remove yourself from the madness so that you will be able to calmly watch the hook float by.

Remember that bullies don't like their anger any more than you do. Oh yes, they use their anger to get what they want. But they are not as happy about it as you might think.

> Bullies are fighting to achieve an altered state of consciousness, rather than to get you to *do* anything in particular...The way to win is to do something unexpected that will jolt Bullies out of their familiar, primitive pattern and make them think about what's going on. They hate that, because it spoils their high.[3]

Ask for time to think. Staying cool, using your mind, and remaining detached is very hard if the aggressor is coming at you fast and furious. You may need to ask for time to consider what is happening. You may have to step away from the situation to gain a more accurate perspective. You may have to raise your hand, gesturing, as you say, "Time out. I need to stop this conversation." The aggressor won't like this—it interrupts his manipulations—but it is healthier for you. If you don't like all the hooks floating by, get out of the water!

Ask them to lower their voice and to speak more slowly. Remaining calm when someone else is agitated can be quite empowering. As you remain under control and ask them to lower their voice, you set the tempo of the encounter while managing your own inner anxiety at the same time. If the aggressor does not do as you ask, separate yourself from him immediately.

Never defend yourself. I thank John Bradshaw, author of *Healing the Shame That Binds You,* for enlightening me about "the shame bind." Bradshaw explains how critical people can hook us into defending our position, thereby reinforcing the "bind." When attacked, however, we seem genetically wired to offer umpteen reasons that explain why the attacker's words are not true. Does that stop them from bombarding us with yet another attack? No. In fact, the result is quite the opposite.

This technique is potent for dealing with any form of criticism or attack. It is actually something you don't do, as opposed to something you do. Standing and listening to the aggressor will bring about greater benefits than defending yourself. Here's how you can achieve this:

First, agree with them. Yes, you heard me right. Agree with them, or at least agree partially. I'm sure you're wondering what I mean, so let's go back to Chuck and me. As he ranted and raved about the state overreacting to his situation, I said, "You know, Chuck, I can hear how upset you are about someone taking your son away. It must feel like people are acting inappropriately by stepping into your business and taking your child. It must feel like meddling to you. I suspect I'd feel the same way."

"Like I said, I'll bet you'd react the same way in my situation," he replied.

"Maybe not exactly the same way, but I'd sure be upset. I'd probably feel like fighting anyone who stood between me and my sons, even if I knew that wasn't the best thing to do."

Did I give up any ground by taking this approach? No. Did I lie to him or tell him something that was not the truth? No. I simply empathized with him and let him know that I understood some of what he was feeling. After I agreed, at least in principle, with his plight, Chuck slowly calmed down. When others escalate, our response should be to de-escalate. When they use their primitive brains, we must use our advanced brains. When they spit and kick, we need to calmly tell them we won't talk to them while they're having a temper tantrum.

Second, remember that fighting off hooks is never easy business. Whatever you do, don't hold your breath and wait for hook-shaking to get easy. It has never happened that way for me. It takes concentration, understanding, and practice.

As you practice these techniques you can expect to become more proficient at avoiding the hook. However, with so many aggressors in our lives, we must recognize that this will be an ongoing battle.

Getting Hooked by the Egotist

If you've been hooked by the aggressor, you've probably been hooked by the egotist as well—they're cousins and often hang out together. Don't be fooled, however. Just because they know each other does not mean that they're friends. They pick fights with one another as often as they pick fights with you.

Let's review what we know about egotists—commonly known as narcissists or self-centered jerks. Here are a few of their traits:

- They believe the world revolves around them.
- They're so caught up in their world that they forget about yours.
- Consequently, they forget others' birthdays, anniversaries and special occasions.
- They show off.
- They brag and exaggerate shamelessly.
- They lack empathy or understanding for others.
- They crave your adulation.
- Under the right circumstances, they can accomplish great things and can even be great leaders.

Remember that egotism and self-esteem are not the same. In fact, egotists often experience flagging self-esteem. They feel a sense of discomfort that compels them to accomplish more, talk more, and strive to be more. Bernstein refers to egotists as narcissists.

> Narcissists evoke mixed feelings. We love their accomplishments, but hate their conceit. We deplore the way they ignore our needs, yet unconsciously we respond to the infants inside them that need us so much. And we need them. Without narcissists, who would lead us? Or who, for that matter, would think themselves wise enough to say where leadership ends and narcissism begins?[4]

The Scriptures tell us, "Do not think of yourself more highly than you ought, but rather think of yourself with sober judgment, in accordance with the measure of faith God has given you" (Romans 12:3). But egotists never heed this advice.

Because of that thing called *denial,* egotists presume this Scripture has nothing to do with them. And their denial is one of the primary ways they hook us. They have no idea how grandiose, how preposterous, they are at times. Because of their lack of empathy, their lack of rapport, they cannot see how hurtful they are to others. In fact, their actions seem normal to them. Egotists commonly barge ahead, trampling feelings along the way without their awareness.

Another major mechanism egotists use to hook us is entitlement. The easiest way to understand this concept is to think about adolescents. I just finished raising two sons, so this is familiar territory for me.

Joshua and Tyson, now 25 and 27, respectively, would come home from school, drop their coats and books on the floor, head straight for the refrigerator, and pull out anything they could put in a sandwich. After making their sandwiches, they left their mustard and mayonnaise jars on the counter, presuming that the fairy maid would swoop down and clean up after them. After all, they'd gone to school that day. They were entitled to eat whatever they wanted with no obligation to clean up after themselves. And heaven forbid that they would express gratitude for their many blessings in life!

Not surprisingly, their behavior didn't sit well with me. When I asked them to clean up their mess, they would become irritated and promise to clean up later, which of course never arrived. Why? You know the answer—because they were entitled. Privileged. Important. Above the trivial matters of life.

The real problem here was not that they simply felt entitled. It was that *I* didn't believe they were entitled, thereby causing friction, tension, and some pretty ugly squabbles. Thankfully, years later, they grew out of this phase that is so common to adolescence. They matured through life experiences and the movement of God in their lives. Keep in mind, however, that not everyone grows out of it. Not everyone is willing to let God change his or her character.

You may work with, socialize with, or live with people who

have not grown out of this immature phase of development. They do not know the meaning of reciprocity—the idea that if you do something nice for me, I will do something nice for you, which is the very basis for creating a balanced relationship. They still believe they shouldn't have to wait in line, shouldn't have to pay full price, shouldn't ever get stuck in a traffic jam, shouldn't be criticized, and shouldn't have to pick up after themselves. This is the myopic life of the entitled egotist.

Exactly how do they hook you? The entitled egotist needs someone willing to put up with their antics. The most powerful hook for egotists is their tendency to find people who are weaker. People who doubt themselves are attracted to those who have an air of certainty. These people with large doses of charm and charisma are able to make us feel like the second most important individuals in the world. For some of us, this feels pretty good.

Take a moment and picture the biggest egotist you know. Maybe it's the shrewd businessman in your networking group. Maybe it's your child's teacher or perhaps even your pastor. Now, consider the personality of egotists' mates, who are usually far more passive than the egotists. They are more docile, less dominant, and willing to shower the egotists with the admiration they crave. In return, they secretly enjoy some of the benefits of the heralded and hated egotist. By association, they are also the center of attention.

Flinging Back the Hook

Amazingly, a salmon can, in a blur of its head and fins, "throw a hook." Seemingly caught and ready for the grill, the great fighting fish can maneuver its body so the hook is released from its mouth and it is free once again.

Because egotists are so powerful, so convincing, throwing their hook is difficult. Doing so requires a great deal of moxie.

Remember, egotists like to be with people who are mesmerized by their leadership. They thrive on the dominant-passive relationship, regardless of how much they deny it. Egotists seek weaker people who are disconnected from themselves. Patricia Evans, author of

Controlling People, describes those who are most easily caught by the egotist.

> Having learned to deny their own wisdom and having taken in other people's definitions of them, without even realizing it, those who are disconnected from themselves construct an identity not grounded in experience but constructed out of, or in reaction to, other people's ideas, expectations and values.[5]

Because egotists gain their power and influence from our mesmerized view of them, we must break the spell. We must end their manipulation. But how?

Notice the hook. Yep. There it is again—notice the egotists' powerful presentation. Watch the smooth set-up, the deceptive delivery, and finally, the powerful pitch. Keep smiling as you see their need to be front and center. Giggle to yourself, if you'd like, at how juvenile they often are in their approach. They are so transparent, but they don't even know it. Then imagine their next step.

I recall Jake from the business network party that Christie and I hosted. He moved around the room, mingling with the guests. He was not just mingling, however. He was strutting like a peacock, setting the stage, building rapport in his delivery, and finally, making his pitches. He was slipping people his business cards and expecting them to be as grateful as if he were passing out Starbucks coffee cards.

Stop fishing. Get out of the river. You can't get hooked if you're not in the water. Practically speaking, you can't get hooked if you don't need the bait. You need to define your own identity from the inside out rather than letting the egotist tell you what you are thinking, feeling, and wanting. You must spend time prayerfully deciding what is most important in your life. By doing so, you actively create a new self that knows its own identity.

I am working with a 50-year-old woman named Sandy, a charming person with a quick wit. Divorced twice, both times from egotists, she has struggled to rebuild her identity. Since her painful divorces, however, Sandy has gone back to college to finish her degree. She now teaches third grade and has a group of friends with whom she travels in the summers. She sings in her church's choir and has resumed piano lessons after a 20-year hiatus. She is considering dating again.

Sandy is frightened about dating because she fears she might again be attracted to egotists. "I wonder," she says, "if I have learned anything. I know myself a lot better, and know I don't want someone to tell me how to dress, what to think, and what I need to do to be the perfect wife. I want someone who will honor me for who I am."

I applaud the work Sandy has done in her life. I point out the changes she has made and help her see how different she is now from the days when she could be defined, manipulated, and controlled by egotists. Sandy is well on her way to defining and placing a higher value on herself. She is creating a wonderful opportunity to date in a healthy way and find a man willing to love her. Her fears have not vanished—she has to practice discovering that she can attract healthier men.

Call it a worm. Egotists have a way of luring us into accepting their stories and buying their stuff, even when we don't want it. It's okay to smile and acknowledge the value of their bait. We might go along with their charismatic position and nod our heads in agreement, even if we don't agree.

But it's time to call a worm a worm. It's not filet mignon. It's not roast duck. It's just a worm. Jake's business card was just that, a business card—not a gift from the gods. Call it what it is. Practice, one small step at a time, disagreeing with egotists and speaking your truth. It's okay to tell egotists you don't want what they're selling. You won't melt into a big blob on the floor.

The Slickest Salesman

When I think of a charismatic, egotistical, snake-oil salesman with a really big hook, one comes to mind—Satan. Consider his setup, delivery, and ultimate pitch to Jesus—the One who shows us how to resist.

"Then Jesus was led by the Spirit into the desert to be tempted by the devil. After fasting forty days and forty nights, he was hungry. The tempter came to him and said, 'If you are the Son of God, tell these stones to become bread'" (Matthew 4:1-3). Satan is very clever and tries to prey upon Jesus' vulnerability from hunger. Jesus, however, is firm and unswerving and refuses to fall for his ploy. But the slick salesman tries again.

"Then the devil took him to the holy city and had him stand on the highest point of the temple. 'If you are the Son of God,' he said, 'throw yourself down.'" Satan tempts Jesus to gain public attention through spectacle rather than through His righteous life, but again Jesus resists this temptation. He knows who He is. He is clear about His purpose and mission. He is sure about His identity.

Satan takes Jesus to a mountaintop and shows Him all the kingdoms of the world and their splendor. "All this I will give to you if you bow down and worship me." The smooth operator offers Jesus the world, but Jesus is not hooked by this bait. He rebukes Satan and resists his temptations.

A review of this encounter shows Satan throwing out his best lures to Jesus. He is resourceful and manipulative, even to the point of quoting Scripture. He tempts Jesus at a time, and in a particular way, where the bait may have tasted quite good. But the Son of God is victorious.

Jesus is our ultimate example of assuredness. Though lured by temptations of immediate gratification, power, and adulation, He resists. We see through Jesus' encounter with Satan that we can deal courageously with egotists. Certain of our identity, knowing that we have the power of Christ within, we can stand firm, not only against the aggressors and egotists of this world, but against Satan himself.

"Submit yourselves, then, to God. Resist the devil, and he will flee from you. Come near to God and he will come near to you" (James 4:7-8).

This is truly the way.

6

The Big Hook: Borderlines, Sufferers, and Control Freaks

There are those who dance to the rhythm
that is played to them, those who only dance
to their own rhythm, and those who don't dance at all.

JOSE BERGAMIN

September 11 changed our lives forever.

As with the bombing of Pearl Harbor or the assassination of President Kennedy, you probably know exactly where you were and what you were doing when you heard the news of those jets careening into the Twin Towers in New York.

On September 11, 2001, I was with my youngest son, Tyson, on the southern coast of Italy. One moment, we were strolling the streets of Sorrento. The next, we were anxiously huddled around a television set with locals and foreigners, trying to make sense of this terrible act.

We were baffled. Commandeered jets slamming into buildings in downtown New York? Another hijacked plane crashing into the Pentagon? We wondered if we were watching some high-tech Steven Spielberg movie. This craziness could not be real.

93

But it was real. It has taken years to put the pieces of the puzzle together—although many still don't fit into a nice, neat package.

We had been attacked. The United States was in a state of emergency. For Tyson and me, the situation quickly become personal. As Americans in Italy, we had critical questions that needed answering: Could we still travel freely and safely to other cities in Europe, or would we need to get home at once? Could we even get home? We were traveling on American Airlines—the company that owned the downed airliners. We knew that chaos and disruption would dominate the travel industry for some time.

After being bombarded with visuals of the towers crumbling in flames, we went to a café to sort things out. But it was too much information, too dramatic, too frightening. There would be no way to get the answers we needed. We discovered that there were simply too many problems to overcome with a simple phone call.

Our answers were slow in coming. The State Department was, understandably, overwhelmed with questions similar to ours. We waited days for answers, feeling desperately in limbo, considering our options. We finally received instructions—flights would soon be leaving the country, and we were strongly encouraged to take one. A week later we arrived home safely. Home never felt so good.

The kind of disruption and disorientation that Tyson and I felt for that week is similar to what those entangled with crazy-makers face every day. In the previous chapter we reviewed how the aggressor and egotist create chaos in our world, driving us crazy. Let's now explore together the crazy-making hooks used by three other crazy-makers—the borderline, the sufferer, and the control freak.

Talk to a man married to a borderline, another of our crazy-makers, who struggles with unexpected eruptions on a daily basis. Ask him what it is like to constantly try to make sense of what is happening. Listen to him try to explain the emotional roller coaster of his married life. He racks his brain to determine what he could have possibly done to warrant the latest treatment he received from his mate. He attempts in vain to understand the borderline's over-reaction to every minor problem. But nothing makes sense.

Ken is fit and trim, 45 years old, a successful businessman married to Katherine, an equally successful attorney. Both have been gifted with intellect, financial stability, three gorgeous children, and a large home in the upscale suburbs of Seattle.

Ken is a middle manager in a computer software business. There is little he doesn't know about computers, software, information systems, and running a business. But Ken's brilliance provides no help in understanding his wife. His education and training did nothing to prepare him for the daily exam he faces in Borderline Management 101.

Katherine has repeatedly humiliated Ken with her mouthy outbursts, twisted and distorted thinking, and unfair accusations. On many occasions, he has threatened to leave her. He has spent many nights on the couch and a few at a local motel, and he has consulted an attorney about divorce. Ken is a Christian who takes his marriage vows very seriously. He loves his children, but his world is chaotic, unpredictable, and unstable. He is miserable. When he came to me for counseling, he tearfully told me the following story.

"I'm not sure what to do. I met Katherine as a starry-eyed, young man at a small Christian college in the Midwest. She was so full of life and on fire for the Lord. I was kind of an egghead; she was spontaneous and playful. I was a tightwad; she convinced me it was all right to spend money. Those were great days."

"When did things begin to change?"

"After our whirlwind courtship, I saw an immediate difference in Katherine's behavior. Little things rocked her world. She got angry for no reason and blamed everything on me. I was shocked at first and wondered if I was making this up. Maybe I finally started to see her for who she really was."

"And things have never gotten better?"

"My life has been one nightmare after another. I know it's going to sound like I'm making this stuff up, but I'm not. Katherine is moody. Life is wonderful one minute; the next minute, she freaks out on me, on the kids, on anybody in her path. She has an explosive temper and can say mean things. Maybe her ruthlessness makes her a good attorney, but it definitely doesn't make her a good wife or mother. Every time I think I can't take it, things improve temporarily. She backs off a little, and I remember why I married her. Then things go backward, and I'm sick of it again."

Ken went on to talk about how dealing with his wife was much like dealing with their children. He described Katherine as unpredictable, volatile, and immature.

Eruptions occurred without provocation. Small things became large. Trivial concerns became reasons to end their marriage. And when Ken tried to discuss an issue, Katherine's response was to blame others. She could accept no responsibility for the hostility in their relationship.

Getting Hooked by the Borderline

Dealing effectively with a borderline without getting hooked is an arduous task, but you can do it.

Marsha Linehan, a renowned authority on the borderline, offers invaluable advice in her book *Cognitive Behavioral Treatment of Borderline Personality Disorder.*[1] Linehan explains how borderlines struggle intensely with loving and hating the same person, often condemning those with whom they are irritated. Linehan tells us that borderlines struggle with managing their emotions, tolerating stress, and finding practical ways to soothe their troubled lives.

Let's look closely at the mechanisms borderlines use to hook you.

The borderline is particularly adept at making you feel crazy. She (because the majority of borderlines are female, I will use feminine pronouns) employs a defense mechanism known as *projection* to rid herself of unacceptable traits by projecting them onto you. "I don't do such and such; you do," a borderline will say. "I'm not at fault; you are." And so it goes. By projecting their unwanted qualities onto you, masterfully shifting the blame, they never have to be held responsible for their actions or feelings.

Those in relationship with borderlines quickly discover they must walk on eggshells. If not careful, an eruption may occur at any time for any reason. And if the eruption happens, it will never be the borderline's fault.

Having discovered the fragility of the relationship, those closely connected to borderlines are often plagued with self-doubt:

- Could I have handled that situation differently?
- Did I do something wrong?
- Do I deserve this attack on me?
- Am I at fault for what is happening?

Having been hooked by the borderline's use of projection, you may begin to question reality. Distinguishing what is being projected and what is being distorted becomes more and more difficult. Getting hooked means we doubt our view of reality and question whether we are the crazy ones.

First the borderline has you questioning your sanity, and next she makes you feel wrong about yourself. Her strategy is very clear—attack you and your thinking. Often very bright, the borderline can dissect your thinking quickly and effectively. She can find miniscule faults in your views, cracks in what you consider to be solid logic, causing you to reel like a boxer bouncing off the ropes. She makes you wonder what hit you.

Consider this scenario: There you are, minding your own business, when your wife, boss, or colleague comes in and attacks you. You thought you knew what you knew, but she tells you otherwise. You thought you were on solid footing, but she tells you that you have messed up in some way. You were certain of your perceptions, but she tells you those perceptions are wrong.

Frantically, you defend yourself. And that is mistake number one. You have been hooked! You try to convince the borderline that what she is seeing, what she is feeling, what she is perceiving is wrong. But defending yourself does not work. Give it up.

The borderline will also hook you with her intense emotionality. Oh sure, the issue is that she cannot find her car keys, a seemingly trivial matter. But to her, you have been irresponsible with her keys and have created a crisis for her. Do you see how it works? Her emotional crisis becomes your emotional crisis.

How does this hook you? If you believe you can calm her down, you will be hooked. If you think you can use logic to quell her anxiety, think again. You'll be wasting your time and energy.

Besides making you feel wrong, borderlines can hook you with their scattered thinking. If you believe that their argument does not seem logical, you're probably right. It isn't logical. It isn't sequential. In fact, it is probably circuitous, tangential, rambling, and distorted. Still, all your efforts to put it into a nice, neat package will be for naught.

You'll flounder about, hook firmly implanted, trying desperately to make sense of the issue at hand. It won't work because often there is no logic to latch onto. The more attached you are to making sense of the matter, the further you will be pulled in. The more you try to sort out borderlines' thinking, forcing it to set neatly on the table in front of you, the more control they will have over you.

Flinging Back the Hook

Like the mighty salmon, you must find the strength and strategies to throw the hook or, better yet, avoid getting hooked in the first place. Take a moment to consider the following techniques.

Develop detachment. To survive and thrive with a borderline, you must develop the ability to love from a distance. You must develop an ability to observe the drama without participating in it. Much like watching a sitcom on television, you need to watch events unfold without taking them personally.

You can avoid the emotion by consciously creating a layer of protection. Much like putting on the full armor of God, as discussed by the apostle Paul in Ephesians 6, we stand firm against the wiles of the borderline. We stand outside their tactics, confident in our ability to know what we know, feel what we feel, and think what we think. This can't take away the entire sting, but it can help you not to feel crazy.

Own your reality. Rather than owning the perceptions of the borderline, we must own our own reality. Gary Chapman explains this in his book *Loving Solutions.*

> Reality living requires that we take responsibility for our own attitudes. A verbally abused spouse must first of all refuse to believe the negative messages of the verbally abusing husband/wife. We must come to affirm our own worth in spite of the negative messages we are receiving from our spouses. Only as we come to see ourselves as persons of worth and value will we be able to take positive steps which have the potential of changing our marriage relationships.[2]

Give up trying to understand. Yes, this goes completely against our grain. Many of us wrongly believe that if we can understand something, we can control it. But you can't possibly fully understand the thinking of the borderline. If you get hooked trying to understand it, you will simply end up suffering.

Give up your need for consistent love and approval. If you must have the borderline's constant love and approval, you'll forever have a hook in your lip. You must let go of the need for constant approval. This does not mean you can't get love and approval some of the time, but it will not always be available to you unless the borderline seeks in-depth help and healing.

It is important to recognize that borderlines demand attention and an escape from responsibility. This means that if you are close by, you'll be the recipient of their rejection, negative feelings, and blame. If you need their approval, you'll be flailing on the hook indefinitely.

Set limits. You may doubt your ability to set healthy limits. You may feel strange and awkward as you practice detaching, giving up the need to fully understand the borderline. But you can do it. You can determine how you will interact with borderlines, not allowing them to control you. You can discover ways of avoiding the hook altogether. Here's what Randi Kreger says in her book *Stop Walking on Eggshells:*

The secret is deciding beforehand what your limits are, what to do whenever they are not observed, and to be consistent in the process…The problem is that line is too close to the "breaking point"—that line that, if crossed, will lead to drastic consequences. What you need to do is clarify what behavior you will and won't accept, and observe your boundaries.[3]

We will talk in a future chapter about when to leave a crazy-making relationship. Setting limits means just that—a time may come when you will set difficult boundaries. You may withdraw emotionally as a consequence to harmful behavior. You might have to physically leave a relationship, temporarily or permanently.

Love and honor. You will be tempted to take on the role of the victim and remain angry with the borderline. But as Christians, that is not our highest calling. Although we are not called to be abused, we *are* called to love the unlovely and care for those who hurt us. We are called to offer grace, kindness, and respect to everyone. In assessing the characteristics of the abusive mate, Gary Chapman offers us this recipe:

Love says, "I care about you too much to sit here and let you destroy me and yourself. I know that is not for your good and I will not cooperate in the process." Love takes constructive action for the benefit of the one loved regardless of how difficult the action may be.[4]

Matthew 22:39 says, "Love your neighbor as yourself." This is not optional. It is a requirement. We are not designed to passively endure abuse. God calls us to honor ourselves as much as we honor others.

Getting Hooked by the Sufferer

How could we get hooked by someone who is syrupy sweet, movingly mournful, or dutifully depressed? This would at first appear to be an oxymoron. Sufferers can't hook us, we reason. They are down on their luck, discouraged about their pitiful future, and suffering from life's terrible blows. We should feel sorry for them, right? If we are angry, impatient, and annoyed with them, perhaps we are not as loving as we should be.

Although this might be our initial reasoning, closer inspection reveals that our annoyance makes perfect sense. In fact, feeling nutty when confronted with this unique brand of crazy-maker is not at all uncommon. Just what are we responding to that makes us feel so crazy? Let's take a closer look.

One of sufferers' primary hooks is their need. Yes, sufferers desperately need you—to manage their lives, to make them happy, to fix their problems, to be miserable when they are miserable.

They need you—without qualification or reservation, over and over again.

You can easily ascertain that they are unable to effectively manage their lives and are asking for help from you. Sensing this need and not wanting them to be miserable, you rush in to meet their need. The problem is, this gets very tiring after a while.

I recall working professionally with an older, single woman named Donna who was referred to me by her physician. She had sought help for a variety of medical problems. She had back problems and arthritis in one knee, which restricted her mobility. She was also more than 50 pounds overweight. Her physical problems were a concern, but her physician sensed a bigger issue was compounding her physical ailments: her anger over the fact that her three adult children no longer had any interest in visiting her.

Donna was depressed and wore her frustrations about life on her sleeves. To make matters worse, she was an extremely reluctant participant in the counseling process, preferring to attribute her anger and depression to her "ungrateful children." When I encouraged Donna to examine why her children no longer visited her, she was unable to offer any plausible explanations other than their ingratitude.

Our conversations during the next few weeks made clear to me, though not to her, that her children avoided her because of her all-consuming needs. She not only had significant issues but also refused to appropriately deal with them, choosing instead to suffer. With something always wrong with her and no apparent solutions on the horizon, she slowly drove away her children and friends. Donna was a downer. Even those who loved her felt crazy in her presence.

Donna could have been a cousin to another type of sufferer known as "poor me." You know them—their problems are always overwhelming. They will never find a job, never find a partner, never have enough money, and worst of all, never get themselves out of their horrible mess.

Sufferers often use "poor me" to hook those who feel a need to rescue others. A magnet seems to draw those who are needy to those who need people to need them. It is a complementary relationship.

Many people complain about their needy, helpless friends, but the rescuer usually experiences some secondary gain. A long pattern of unhealthy interaction has probably been taking place. It looks like this:

- You're a pessimist; I'm an optimist.
- You can't find any solutions for your life; I can help you find the answers.
- You're lost; I'll show you the way.
- You're a follower; I'm a leader.
- You feel unimportant; I feel important.
- You need rescuing; I like rescuing people.

Can you see the hook? Does anyone in your life call incessantly, asking for help? Do you find yourself in the rescuer mode but at times resenting it? Are you getting tired of always carrying the heaviest part of the load? If so, you're in good company. Many folks become entangled with sufferers in one way or another.

Although we'd like to think that sufferers are a distinct group of crazy-makers separate from the rest of us, many of us play a substantial role in their lives. In fact, Stephen Karpman has documented a triangle that occurs with sufferers called the *drama triangle*.

Karpman says the drama triangle is a particularly unique hook. Many counselors believe that we learn in our family of origin whether we are going to be most comfortable in one of three positions: persecutor, rescuer, or victim (sufferer). Our starting position in this triangle is generally set up in childhood. For example, if a parent is overly protective, the child grows up feeling incapable of tackling new situations and is set up for a lifetime role as victim. Or the opposite could occur, with the child taking on the persecutor role and attacking those who don't automatically take care of him.

The hook in this triangle is that everyone needs each other: Victims need someone to save them, the rescuers need someone to fix, and the persecutors need someone to blame. People in a dysfunctional family or marriage feel pressured to take on one of these roles. One of the rescuer's greatest fears is that nobody will be there for them. They encourage dependency in others, thereby making themselves indispensable and avoiding any feelings of abandonment.

Sadly, victims or sufferers often learn to deny their own problem-solving abilities. They tend to see themselves as too weak and fragile to handle life. They seek someone who will rescue and fix them. However, because they are really unfixable, and are entrenched in their "poor me" position, attempts to help them are often thwarted.

How do you feel when you try to help someone, only to find that all your efforts are in vain? What happens in a relationship when whatever you do is not enough? Regardless of how many solutions you offer, none quite fit the bill. None lift sufferers out of their misery. You must ultimately look in the mirror and be candid with yourself—you cannot heal this person. You need not feel guilty about his or her dysfunction.

Sufferers often compound their miserable situations. They frequently heap burning coals of guilt on your head because, in their eyes, you are not doing enough for them. The rescuer in you will struggle to step up and lend a hand, but it won't work. You cannot do enough for those friends to bring them out of their depression. You cannot visit your parents enough to bring a smile to their faces. Regardless of what the issue is, you cannot do enough, and if you're not careful, you will feel like you are not enough.

I have a college friend who is a card-carrying sufferer. Doug is in midlife now and is single again, for the third time. What Doug doesn't seem to realize is that he wears people out. He is an emotional drain on everyone around him. I reluctantly call him to check in, knowing he will immediately launch into a tirade about how the world has done him wrong. Invariably, he will have once again lost a job, broken up with a woman, or left a church in despair. When Doug inevitably lets me know that I have it better than he has it, I feel the subtle darts of guilt for having a happy life. I have to work hard at not rescuing him, knowing that my efforts would be futile.

Avoiding the Role of Rescuer

Ignoring the sufferer's hook is not easy. I have a Ph.D. in caretaking and rescuing. I know how to do that. I cannot rebuild an engine, cannot perform surgeries, and have no understanding about chemical or mechanical engineering, but boy, can I rescue. So imagine my dilemma when a need comes floating by. Immediately, I believe I can fix it.

Over the years, I have come up with specific strategies for resisting the lure of the sufferer.

Give up the need to rescue. My first and foremost task in flinging back the hook is giving up my need to rescue sufferers. I must come face-to-face with the messiah in me that wants to fix everyone. I must let go of the arrogance lingering just beneath the surface that whispers, "I have the answers." I must begin by admitting my pompous attitudes, acknowledging that God is God, and I am not.

This is difficult, especially if we insist that our rescuing is justified in light of sufferers' needs. They cannot live without us, we surmise. This is categorically untrue. Sufferers will get along just fine without our rescuing. They will either figure out that suffering is an optional condition or they will reach out to another rescuer.

Detach yourself from their depression. Yes, some sufferers will simply find other people to symbiotically attach to. They will seek willing parties to nurse them along. All the while, if the sufferers are close to you, you will have to endure their guilt trips. But by detaching yourself, these guilt trips become less and less damaging. We can care without caretaking, love without being emotionally entangled.

The process of distancing ourselves from sufferers includes a conscious act of choosing to be around people who give us energy instead of those who drain energy from us. We actively engage in the process of caring for the one beautiful life for which we are responsible—our own.

This counsel is, of course, more difficult if the sufferer is your spouse. How do you detach emotionally from your lover, with whom you live? This is a much more demanding task. It will require more concentration, more prayer, more support, more attention to your health and well-being.

Give back responsibility. Detaching from sufferers can be a biblically sound enterprise. The apostle Paul talks at length in Galatians 6 about responsible behavior. You will note that he says we are to "carry each other's burdens" (Galatians 6:2). These burdens, however, are burdens that they cannot carry alone. They are legitimate burdens, overwhelming circumstances with which people genuinely need help. We are called to help those who have these legitimate challenges. Thus, we choose to volunteer at homeless shelters, work for Habitat for Humanity, and go on medical missions.

A few verses later, however, we discover that "each one should carry his own load" (Galatians 6:5). These are the difficulties in life that we are meant to handle ourselves—perhaps owing to the laws of reaping what we have sown. We are to carry our own load in many circumstances. We should learn to manage numerous challenges in life, knowing that working out solutions, with God's help, makes us stronger. Understand that this position is not only solid, it is biblical. Give the load back to the sufferers. To carry it for them is to enable them to remain weak, helpless, and fragile—and that's not good for them or for you.

Getting Hooked by the Control Freak

As is the case with other crazy-makers, getting hooked by control freaks is all too easy. They are ready and willing to tell us how to do things, why their way is the right way, and why we should do things differently. They are quite willing to leap over any boundaries we have erected to get smack dab in our face and bombard us with the truth.

Standing up against this type of person is difficult, to say the least. If you have fragile boundaries, you're doomed. If you have any questions about your position, your beliefs, or your thoughts, you are in trouble. Let's look more closely at some of the tactics control freaks use to hook us.

Control freaks are very adept at employing criticism. Because control freaks want things to go their way, they resort to criticism in order to seize the upper hand. Their perfectionism is a vice that masquerades as a virtue, and when you don't go along with their way of doing things, you are not only wrong but morally inferior.

Control freaks are absolutely convinced that their way of doing things is the only way. They are close-minded and dogmatic. If you are in relationships with control freaks, you will be hooked if you try to dissuade them from their position. You will get hooked if you try to argue with them—they thrive on confrontation! They are the commanding generals, and everyone is expected to obey their orders.

Control freaks are not only domineering, they are tenacious in their control. They are like a bulldog with a bone—there is absolutely no way you will dissuade them from their point of view. Any attempt to do so will only lead to frustration on your part. They are relentless, narrowly focused, and doggedly determined. They must be right in order to control their underlying anxiety. They fear feeling helpless, vulnerable, and out of control.

Dr. Les Parrott, author of the book *The Control Freak*, says control freaks also hook us with their obnoxious behavior. He explains that control freaks alienate friends, family members, and coworkers with their controlling behavior but are apparently oblivious to their harmful actions.

Control freaks also expect allegiance. They are often shocked if you go against their way of doing things. They have thought through their position and rationalized it as the only way. To not agree is to bruise their fragile ego, sending them into an emotional tailspin. Sensing this, you may tiptoe around them, making concessions you really don't want to make—and you're hooked.

But to go against control freaks means you will incur their wrath—and this can be an intimidating matter. Control freaks possess a bit of the aggressor inside as well. Things are fine as long as you go along with their game plan. To oppose their version of the truth is tantamount to going against God. Their hook, then, is their anger, which we have learned can be frightening.

Resisting the Control Freak's Power Trip

It may be difficult to understand what it is about the control freak's power and dominance that hooks us. After all, who wants to be told how to do things?

Hard as it may seem to believe, some people actually want this kind of control in their lives. They want someone to tell them how to live, eat, and breathe. However, I suspect that you do not belong to that group. You think for yourself and are ready to be the person God created you to be. Let's consider how to fling back the control freak's hook.

Break the spell. Patricia Evans, in her book *Controlling People,* writes at length about the ability of controlling people to put you under their mesmerizing spell. They can be so convincing that you go along with their game plan even though you resent it. So step one is to break their spell. Notice their tactics. Recognize their anxious dogmatism. Observe how they try to make you think the way they think. Be mindful of their narrow focus.

Evans suggests that one great tactic is to cry out, "What?"

She adds, "When I first used it, I didn't think it would be particularly effective. Surely, I thought, I could come up with something really clever. But, now as time has passed, I realize this response is very effective."[5] The tactic stops you from falling under their spell and alerts them that you are not going along with their plan.

Think for yourself. After breaking their spell, you begin the process of thinking for yourself. You question the bill of goods they are trying so desperately to sell you. You say, "I don't agree with you" and notice the difference that makes. Mostly, you want to start the process of identifying yourself as different from the control freak.

Don't debate. Disagreeing with the control freak doesn't mean debating with them. They thrive on verbal warfare, and if you enter that arena, you'll be beaten. Guard against getting into a power struggle with control freaks. They're much more tenacious than you and will outlast you every time. Fling back the hook by refusing to debate with them.

Ask for validation of your perception. After learning to disagree and discovering that you can survive, ask for validation of your point of view. Ask them to state your point of view before launching ahead with their position. Understand that you may not get it, but it's worth a try. You are not asking that they agree with your opinion—only that you have a right to think differently than they think. If you are unable to do this, your relationship is in great danger. The ability to be different is at the heart of our uniqueness and self-worth.

Talk about the control freak's anxiety. Practice addressing the real issues. If your mate is a control freak and is anxious about your faithfulness, talk about it in terms of his anxiety. Share with him that you understand, and hear his concern when he asks about your whereabouts. If your spouse is anxious about money, talk about money in terms of his anxiety. Put the problem back where it belongs—on his shoulders. In fact, affirm that you even understand his anxiety about the matter.

Set healthy boundaries. Learning to set healthy boundaries is a great way of flinging back the hook. You can lovingly tell the control freak that you will be doing things the way you prefer to do them, not the way he wants. Learn to say no to small demands. When your mother tells you to be there by five o'clock, tell her you'll be able to be there by five thirty. When your boyfriend demands that you account for where you were this afternoon, tell him you are not going to answer to him. Find small ways to make it clear that you are a separate individual.

Freedom

Being hooked is the definitive form of bondage. To be hooked is to completely lose your freedom. Whether you are hooked by the antics of the borderline, the passive-aggressiveness of the sufferer, or the tenacious power plays of the control freak, you lose autonomy and joy. We were created for liberty, not captivity and oppression. Christ provides appropriate advice about this subject.

> The Spirit of the Lord is on me, because he has anointed me to preach good news to the poor. He has sent me to proclaim freedom for the prisoners and recovery of sight for the blind, to release the oppressed, to proclaim the year of the Lord's favor (Luke 4:18).

Jesus was quoting from Isaiah 61:1-2, where Isaiah imagines the deliverance of Israel from exile in Babylon. But the release from Babylonian exile had not brought the emotional and spiritual freedom the people expected; they were still a conquered and oppressed nation. Isaiah was referring to the coming of Christ as their ultimate source of sovereignty. Isaiah pictured freedom as an internal spiritual condition that affected external circumstances.

I don't know about you, but I crave independence. I want my life controlled by the Spirit of God, the author of the good news. Instead of captivity, I crave freedom. Instead of blindness, I desire clear vision. Isaiah's words were true for the children of Israel, and they're just as true for us today. Whatever you are experiencing, God is the author of peace in the midst of any storm, including crazy-making. I encourage you to practice the principles in this chapter and claim His promise of freedom.

7

The Net of Deception

Nothing is easier than self-deceit. For what each man
wishes, that he also believes to be true.

Demosthenes

The Scriptures tell us, "You will know the truth, and the truth will set you free" (John 8:32).

But what happens if we are not completely truthful with ourselves and others? In a world of deception and distortion, conversations are labored, words are twisted, and emotions are exaggerated. Relationships become chaotic. This world of deception is home to our crazy-makers.

I am reminded of annual trips to the carnival as a youth. I especially remember the house of mirrors. In a moment, simply by passing through a set of doors, I entered another world. Everything was instantly distorted. Fat people grew fatter, faces became twisted and gnarled, and my sense of reality was completely disrupted.

At one time or another, we have all been in relationships where truthfulness was replaced by distortion. In these situations, we often experience anxiety associated with suddenly losing our sense of reality. This is what crazy-makers can do to us.

Crazy-makers live in a world of deception that is quite natural to them. They invite you into that world, and once you are there, you are easily caught. The fact that we care about these people makes us especially vulnerable.

The truth sets us free, but deception keeps us in bondage. When we allow ourselves to get caught up in the crazy-makers' distortions, we no longer have the ability to make healthy choices. We are enslaved because we see things as we wish them to be or as the crazy-makers wish them to be but not as they truly are. Just as in a house of mirrors, everything is distorted. It's enough to make us scream for a dose of reality.

To seek and to tell the truth is a virtuous undertaking. I don't believe I have ever fully done either one. Oh, I'd like to come across as righteous by telling you that I am always a truth teller. Unfortunately that would not be the truth. I am much more comfortable living in a world of half-truths that I tell myself and others. Even when seeking the truth, I desire it in small doses, and only if it is not too painful. I know that the truth may demand changes I am not ready to make.

For months, if not years, after my painful divorce, I told myself I was trying to learn from my mistakes. I read books about divorce, attended a divorce recovery program, and even spoke to singles groups about rebounding from divorce. I told myself I wanted to face issues head-on. But that wasn't the complete truth. Rigorous honesty is challenging, demanding; and even now I live in a partial cloak of deception. Rigorous honesty demands we confront our own weaknesses and sins.

When I am fiercely honest with myself, which is the only path that leads to healing and healthy relating, I admit that I don't want to face my role in the divorce. I want to blame my ex for every problem that occurred in our marriage. I also want others to blame her and find fault with her actions while holding me blameless. I want people to feel sorry for me, to remember that I didn't want the divorce. The problem is that I'm not willing to let the spotlight of truth shine on me.

So I avoid reality. I don't tell people that my workaholism, always under the guise of being a good provider, played a significant role in the failure of my marriage. It is painful to admit that I was absent during much of my children's formative years. I don't want anyone to know about the excessive discipline I used with my sons, which caused unnecessary tension in my marriage.

When I finally get around to being candid with myself, I am forced to acknowledge that I have repeatedly used manipulation and distortion to avoid the truth about my performance as a husband and father.

Perhaps you can relate. Perhaps, like me, you prefer to dodge the intense light of scrutiny.

The Importance of Truth

As manipulative as I can be when covering up my failures, crazy-makers cast an even broader net of deception. They simply cannot tolerate looking honestly at their condition, and when you associate with them, you can fall victim to their trickery.

We must understand this crucial principle if we are to interact in any healthy way with crazy-makers. We must recognize that most lack the ability to be aware of, and sensitive to, their deception.

It's called denial.

Maintaining my innocence in the divorce fools no one. Others know I am far from perfect and that I contributed to the destruction of my marriage. To invest energy in the ruse simply prevents me from being honest with others and myself.

Consider the importance of truth. Consider how our society and our faith are built upon the presumption that we need to be truthful with ourselves and others. When anyone in a relationship is dishonest, the integrity of that relationship is compromised. The relationship becomes dysfunctional.

Scott Peck speaks about this issue in his book *The Road Less Traveled*.[1] He offers the following guidelines for us to follow.

First, never speak falsehoods. As you might imagine, this is easier said than done. Nonetheless, it is an important principle. Peck suggests making it a core value in your relationships. Tell the truth.

Second, bear in mind that the act of withholding the truth is always a potential lie. We sometimes act virtuous about not lying, when to withhold truth is also an act of deception. When we pretend that we agree with something, we are being deceptive. When we withhold truth from someone who really needs to hear the truth, we do them no favors. We merely enable deception to continue.

Third, the decision to withhold the truth should never be based on personal needs, such as a need for power, a need to be liked, or a need to protect oneself from challenge. How often do we fear sharing our truth because we may be criticized for it? How often do we stop short of the truth because someone might be offended? Dancing around an issue is often easier and far safer. Better to be liked, we reason, than to risk having someone upset with us.

Fourth, the decision to withhold the truth must always be based upon the needs of the people from whom the truth is being withheld. Peck suggests that we base our decisions about truth telling on the needs of the other, not our own comfort level. Most often we base our decisions on how we will feel telling the person the truth. We may tell ourselves, *They can't handle hearing this truth,* when in reality, we do not want to face our own fears. We want to avoid the tension often accompanying truth telling.

Fifth, the assessment of another's needs is an act of responsibility so complex that it can only be executed wisely when one operates with genuine love for the other. To truly consider what is best for others, we must extend ourselves for them. We must truly love them. We dare not act out of malicious intent or desire to harm them. Obviously, telling someone the truth because we are angry with them would not be a wise thing to do.

Sixth, the primary factor in the appraisal of another's needs is the assessment of that person's capacity to utilize the truth for personal spiritual growth. When we tell the truth, we must assess what the receiver might do with that truth. Is he capable of hearing and utilizing it? Is sharing this truth likely to help or hurt him? If we determine the person is truly incapable of utilizing the truth, that to share the information would well be injurious, we must not share it.

Finally, in assessing the capacity of another to utilize the truth for personal spiritual growth, we should remember that our tendency is generally to underestimate rather than overestimate this capacity. Because of our own fear of sharing the truth, we often rationalize our reluctance by thinking that other people can't handle the truth. Peck says that this is usually not the case. I agree.

Why Seek Truth?

You may find yourself wondering if anyone can follow the rules Peck has laid down. Complying to these guidelines for truthfulness is arduous at best and nearly impossible at worst. Subsequently, many people opt for a life of limited honesty—which is certainly true of our cadre of crazy-makers.

Crazy-makers, however, are not the only ones who struggle with honesty. As I mentioned previously, most of us choose to be somewhat deceptive. Like Adam and Eve in the Garden, most of us spend at least some of our time hiding. We don't want others to know the truth about us, so we go to great lengths to present the most positive image of ourselves. Madison Avenue advertising thrives on our need and desire to look good.

Though sometimes difficult, honesty is still the best policy. Why do I believe that? I again offer Scott Peck's counsel.

> The rewards of the difficult life of honesty and dedication to the truth are more than commensurate with the demands. By virtue of the fact that their maps are continually being challenged, open people are continually growing people. Through their openness they can establish and maintain intimate relationships far more effectively than more closed people. Because they never speak falsely they can be secure and proud in the knowledge that they have done nothing to contribute to the confusion of the world, but have served as sources of illumination and clarification.[2]

I propose truth not only because it is morally right and biblically prescribed but also because it makes sense. As Peck says, to speak truthfully adds illumination and clarity to the world.

Truth also sets us free. When we live in the truth, we don't need to hide from anyone. We don't need to slink around in the shadows, fearful of being exposed. We know who we are, we are comfortable in our own skin, we are willing to let others see our shortcomings. We know we have them, so others might as well see them as well. Not that we must expose all of our foibles—we must use wise discernment. Sometimes sharing "too much information" is not helpful, such as when it really is not the other's business to know it.

Deception breeds additional deception. In the Genesis story, we read that Adam and Eve sinned and were ashamed. Instead of coming clean with their sinfulness, they lied about it. In fact, they told lie upon lie, pointing blame in every possible direction—to Satan, to God, and to each other. They tried to hide and cover up their lies, which of course was impossible. The more falsehoods they told, the more they had to continue lying in order to hide their sins.

Deception began in the Garden with Adam and Eve and continues with us today. We inhabit a paradise lost. Just as in the Garden, deception today breeds a world filled with confusion and chaos—and this is where crazy-makers spend the majority of their time.

The truth still sets us free. The truth allows us, as it did Adam and Eve, to come clean with our sin. Being honest with our sin and deficiencies allows us the opportunity to change. It allows God to enable us to recover from wounds and become healthier people.

Crazy-Makers and the Truth

Each of our crazy-makers is skilled in the art of deception, and we need to understand how, and perhaps even why, they rely on deceit. Let's look more closely at how our crazy-makers employ dishonesty and trickery and the impact they have on us.

Aggressors

Aggressors want to avoid the truth at any cost. They are masters at deception. They are prepared to explode in anger if you don't go along with their game plan. For them, it's "my way or the highway."

If aggressors were always aggressive, the choice would be easy—

the highway, of course. But things aren't that simple. A man with antisocial personality disorder—often the underlying diagnostic category of the aggressor—can be as charming as a snake-oil salesman. He can con you out of your money, your home, and your sexuality. The APD man or woman uses deception like a private detective uses eavesdropping equipment to discover information about you that will make you vulnerable.

Consider Stephan, a client referred to me by his attorney for domestic violence treatment. He appeared in my office wearing jeans and a Harley-Davidson T-shirt. He had long salt-and-pepper hair and a handlebar mustache. I judged him to be in his midforties.

He made no effort to impress me. He had been arrested and evicted from his home for slapping his wife during an altercation. It was not his first skirmish with the law, but he insisted it would be his last.

"Let's talk about what happened," I said during his initial evaluation interview.

"There's not much to say," Stephan said. "We were arguing with each other, and things got heated. I slapped her once, she called the cops, and I was arrested. That's it."

Stephan sat rigidly in his chair, arms crossed, cool and collected. His gaze was steady, his speech firm and smooth. Stroking his moustache, he looked at me as if to let me know that the next move was mine.

Stephan's composed exterior seemed like an attempt to control the evaluation, a way to avoid exposing any more of himself than was absolutely necessary. His simple version of the incident would have been more plausible, however, had I not read the police report, which revealed a very different story. That version, complete with testimony from his estranged spouse, strongly suggested Stephan had a history of verbal and physical abuse. She told the officer that Stephan had hit her several times and noted, "He has done this before. If he doesn't get his way he blows up."

As I read the official version of the incident aloud, Stephan kept his gaze steady. "Not true," was his response to each accusation.

"What do you mean?" I asked.

"Not true," he said firmly. "You can believe what you want to believe, but it's not true. I know the game. You're being paid to make me look bad."

Stephan was obviously lying to me. It was quite apparent that there was more to the story than he was willing to reveal. Stephan was an aggressor, fully comfortable with his own deception.

I have worked extensively with aggressors. They often twist the truth to fit their needs at a particular moment. They use fear and intimidation to control others, and it often works. They employ deception and twist words to convince others not to look too closely into their lives or their motives. If necessary, they use outright lies. At times, what they don't say is deceptive. These people are not willing to share any more of the truth than what they can use to their own advantage.

If you challenge an aggressor's thinking or behavior, you aren't likely to get the truth. Aggressors are not likely to own up to their deceptive ways. In fact, they are more likely to dig themselves in even deeper, using more lies to cover up the original deception. They may even attempt to turn the tables on you by accusing you of the very thing of which you have accused them. Stephan used a form of manipulation and truth twisting when he challenged me.

"You're paid to make me look bad," he said. I had to stop for a moment to consider whether any part of that statement was true. Certainly I was being paid for my services, and I profit financially if he is required to seek treatment in my program. Stephan obviously was skilled in the art of manipulation.

But if we open our eyes, we see aggressors for what they are—aggressive, self-centered, and immature. Dr. Paul Meier, in his book *Don't Let the Jerks Get You Down,* calls them "jerks." Others call them bullies and intimidators. Aggressors are people we often choose to avoid—until we are caught in their net of deception and have no choice but to find a way to deal with them.

Egotists

Egotists often hang out with aggressors, though they don't necessarily appreciate one another. They just happen to like the same kinds of people because they are characteristically alike, and that makes for quite a chaotic world. Aggressors are a bit egotistical, and egotists are a bit aggressive.

The egotist, as you will recall, knows everything and everybody. Their egos are so big that when they walk into a room, they suck up most of the air.

Egotists are deceptive because they have an over-inflated view of their worth, their actions, and their thinking. As Dr. Robert Bramson states in his book *Coping with Difficult People,* egotists have

> a tone of absolute certainty, of sureness beyond mortal doubt, that, often without conscious intent, leaves others feeling like objects of condescension… Most frustrating of all is that these insufferable paragons of logic usually turn out to be absolutely right. Thus, they leave others feeling inept, confused, or stupid.[3]

Not surprisingly, egotists are egotistical. They are conceited, boastful, and selfish—and very deceptive. Convinced that their way is the right way, they have little tolerance for other points of view. No wonder you feel smaller when you are around them. You lose energy while they consume it.

Egotists will resort to deceptive tactics to get their way. They demand attention with their brash antics, usurping your ability to have a say in matters. They guide conversations in the direction they want them to go. This is, at the basest level, dishonest. They are ultimately saying, "This is all about me, and you don't matter." Egotists are skilled at manipulating your words and twisting them into their brand of truth. It's all about their agenda.

Dr. Bramson summarizes the deceptive and manipulative nature of egotists: "They don't wait, they don't recycle, they don't pay retail, they don't stand in line, they don't clean up after themselves, they don't let other people get in front of them in traffic, and their income taxes rival great works of fiction."[4]

Egotists cannot be trusted to present the truth to you. They will present their version, which they have manipulated to make themselves look good. This is important to know. When you are dealing with an egotist, you must have your "truth sifter" in hand.

Borderlines

If egotists massage the truth to look good, borderlines manipulate the truth so that they never have to look or feel bad. Relating to borderlines is a most difficult venture, primarily because their version of the truth is so distorted. Having a healthy conversation with them is nearly impossible unless you catch them during one of their rare lucid moments.

You may recall that borderlines tend to have volatile emotions, which hinders them from seeking the truth and having clear, honest communication with others. Many borderlines are "ragers." They can be as explosive and hurtful as aggressors. When raging, they cannot remain clearheaded. They are temperamental, overly sensitive, easily angered, prone to exaggerate problems, and eager to amplify perceived wrongs they have suffered. For borderlines, the sky is always falling.

Borderlines are not openly deceptive. Instead, they are more prone to distort reality. Flooded with unregulated emotion, they approach the world from a childish, self-centered perspective. Like the seven-year-old who throws a tantrum because she is not invited to a birthday party, borderlines take things very personally. They exaggerate the severity of the wrongs done to them, twisting and turning the facts until they are barely recognizable.

Constance came to see me for symptoms of depression amid a background of relational instability. At age 43, she was bright and attractive and took pride in her appearance. College-educated, she worked as a financial analyst for a local firm. But her professional life was faring far better than her personal life.

Constance made an immediate impression. I was ten minutes late to our first session. As I entered the office, she looked at her watch and said, "Will I be receiving my full time today?"

"Of course," I said. "I'm sorry for being late."

"My time is valuable," she replied curtly.

Enough said.

I knew Constance would be exacting and demanding. I would need to be careful not to offend her, and yet to be too careful would be to fall victim to her manipulation. I determined to watch for any patterns of this kind of behavior and for ways I might help her see how this behavior might fit into her ongoing relational problems.

Constance had been divorced twice in the past ten years. She now had custody of her two daughters after a protracted custody battle with her second husband. She told me that this battle "was one I would not let myself lose, and I didn't, even though it took its toll on me emotionally and financially."

"What's the problem?" I asked.

"I met a man a few months ago. He's a wolf in sheep's clothing. I thought he was wonderful at first. Now, after falling in love with him, I find out that he's an alcoholic. He becomes a monster when he drinks."

"Tell me more about your relationship," I said.

"Robert and I met at our church. He seemed like a wonderful man. He was kind and sensitive. My girls love him. But they haven't seen the side of him I've seen. They haven't seen the way he attacks me verbally. It's gotten so bad, we've already broken up three or four times."

"Three or four times in just a few months?"

"I love him and I hate him. Robert can be so kind, so wonderful. But when he drinks, things get crazy. He loses his composure, and I don't do a good job of controlling my temper either."

"Tell me about your temper."

"That's not why I'm here," she said sharply. "I'm here because I'm depressed about our relationship."

"Do you drink with Robert?"

"A little. But as I've already told you, he's the one with the problem. I'm here because I don't know what to do."

"What do you believe your options to be?"

"Well, I love him," she said. "I'm committed to him. But things are so volatile. We can be getting along wonderfully one minute, and then we're screaming at each other the next. It drives me crazy."

"In what way?"

"We end up calling each other names. When he drinks, he gets angry very easily. If I drink a little, we can both get nasty."

"Have you considered that you both might need to get help with the drinking?"

"He said he's already had treatment and knows what he needs to do."

"Do you believe that?" I asked. "It sounds to me like he's in denial. And it sounds like you two have enough problems without alcohol being added to the mix."

"I don't know what to believe," she said. "We get along well when no alcohol is involved. But we both like to have a glass of wine or two when we go out for dinner. I don't really think either of us wants to quit drinking."

"But do you think it's worth the price you are paying?"

"I'll admit that it's a high price. We fight for hours. He threatens to break up with me and stomps out the door. It drains me. I've been through enough breakups. I don't want to go through another one."

I continued to gather information about Constance's history during our following sessions. It was often difficult to determine the truth. Constance had a strong need to present herself as the innocent victim of an aggressive man. However, her story seemed twisted in the direction of portraying her in the most favorable light.

She offered mixed reviews of Robert. But what about her role? Was she also drinking excessively? Did she also have anger problems? What had caused her two divorces, and why had there been such a struggle over who would have custody of her daughters?

Constance exhibited borderline characteristics—intense and volatile emotions, dramatic and troubled relationships, a lack of insight, a tendency to twist things in her favor.

My work was cut out for me as I tried to sift through Constance's stories. Everything she shared with me had a self-serving element. I searched for the truth and some way to help her.

Sufferers

Getting the unvarnished truth from a sufferer can be as difficult as with any other crazy-makers. While less likely to engage in blatant lying, sufferers have an incredible ability to twist the facts in their favor. No one struggles like they do. No one has it as rough. You couldn't possibly understand how horrible their life has been. In fact, according to them, everything works out perfectly for everyone else—the rest of us are the lucky ones.

Sufferers can be much like borderlines in the aspect of truth-twisting, except the sufferer has a corner on whining and playing the victim. Sufferers try to invoke pity from us, whereas borderlines often make us angry. Both make us feel crazy.

Without insight into what makes them tick, trying to help sufferers see how they set themselves up for failure is a thorny enterprise. I don't recommend that you take on the challenge. They will outlast you, outwit you, outthink you.

Sufferers must cling tenaciously to their version of the truth—the truth that makes them the victim of life's cruelty. They do not want to see reality, as empowering as that would be. The truth would set them free, but they don't really want to be free.

If the truth sets us free, it also gives us a mountain of responsibility. For example, if sufferers were to face the facts, they would realize that they always see the glass as half empty. They would discover that they twist facts so they can blame others for their unhappiness, when in fact the sufferers themselves are the key contributors to relational problems. But this insight into the truth would require them to change. And we all know that change is not easy.

Relating to sufferers, who are adrift in the fog of victimhood, is difficult. They are enmeshed in their plight, and they have an incredible ability to catch you in their web. The second you try to convince them that they are not victims, they draw the web around you like a fly in a Venus flytrap. They build their lives around distortion.

The key to not getting caught in their trap is to refuse to buy in to their perception of being victimized. For example, one woman I worked with often received calls from her mother, who wanted to tell her all the wrongs my client's siblings had done to her, their mother. It was always her siblings who had done something wrong, never her mother. My client worked very hard, and successfully, to not get "triangulated" into these conversations, telling her mother she would not talk about her siblings without them being present. She told her mother she did not want to listen to her mother talk badly about her siblings, and in this way freed herself from her mother's deceptive trap.

Control Freaks

Control freaks avoid the truth more than any other crazy-makers, all the while appearing to seek it. Control freaks push and push and push for the truth, but they are completely blinded by the fact that it is their version of the truth that they want.

Dr. Les Parrott, in his book *The Control Freak,* lists ten qualities of the control freak. Consider how each of these characteristics contributes to distortions, leading ultimately to deception. Consider also what it must feel like to be with such a person.

Obnoxious. Control freaks damage nearly every relationship they are in because of their controlling and destructive ways. They push their brand of the truth on others regardless of the cost to the relationship.

Tenacious. Control freaks fiercely hold on to their way regardless of how much resistance this evokes in others. Even when friends, family members, coworkers, and spouses plead with them to explore other options, they are resolute in defense of their perceptions and behavior.

Invasive. Control freaks are so blinded by their perception of the truth, and so anxious to defend it, that they will read their mates' diaries, tap their phone lines, and resort to stalking. Reassurance or explanations seem to have little impact on them.

Obsessive. Control freaks often focus on only one aspect of a problem, losing sight of the bigger picture. They find a single issue that bothers them terribly and hammer away at it, in spite of other, more important matters. Likewise, they focus on other people's faults, losing sight of others' many fine attributes.

Perfectionistic. Control freaks demand perfection of themselves and others. Again, they twist and manipulate the truth to suit their needs.

Criticism. Control freaks believe their criticisms will be received with open arms and will make the situation better. They focus obsessively on a matter, even though it may be trivial, attempting to seek a better way of doing things.

Irritability. Control freaks inevitably fail to reach their desired goals, leaving them irritable and upset—many times alone amid the ruins of a relationship.

Demanding. Control freaks don't simply suggest a different way of doing things. Their way is the *only* way. They have no insight into how their demanding style makes others feel.

Rigid. Trying to have a reasonable conversation with a control freak can be tantamount to bending a piece of steel. They are rigid in their perception of the truth. They hold onto their version of reality even when convincing information is presented to them.

Close-minded. Their mind is made up. Done. Finished. No negotiating. If you happen to succeed in engaging them in negotiations, they will give little and demand a lot, leaving you feeling like the loser in the deal.

Parrott relays the following information about the control freak: "Sadly, many Control Freaks close their mind before they allow good thoughts to enter it. And ultimately, they close their heart to people who would also like to have a place in their life—if only there were room."[5]

Erosion of Integrity

While most of us endorse the concept of honesty, we rarely hold ourselves to the same standard we expect from others. We loathe white lies people tell us, yet we tell them with regularity. We expect others to "speak the truth in love" but are reluctant to do the same ourselves. We hold double standards, which means a bit of the crazy-maker resides in all of us.

Most of us espouse honesty. "Honesty is always the best policy," we proclaim. But our behavior is not always consistent with what we say we believe—about honesty and about spiritual values and practices.

Rather than deliberately attempting to deceive, which is what may come to mind when I mention the word *deception,* we tend to shade the truth. We try to induce a misperception in another. We protect ourselves by embellishing the facts; we leave out details so we look better. We minimize wrongdoing and maximize what we have done right by amplifying another's culpability and downplaying our own responsibility.

The 12-step program has, perhaps more than any other movement, led the way in encouraging rigorous honesty. These groups encourage participants to tell the truth even if it is painful. They say, openly and forcefully, "We're only as sick as our secrets." Even if the information is agonizing or embarrassing, the movement espouses openness. Secrets, they purport, breed shame, and shame erodes self-respect and damages relationships. Openness most often generates acceptance and the dissolution of shame.

John Bradshaw, in his book *Healing the Shame That Binds You,* leads the way in promoting self-disclosure.[6] He fiercely attacks secrets in families—personal and extended—as well as in the larger community. He believes the church needs to become even more real by letting go of facades—the facade of pretending to have it all together when behind the scenes we are struggling with serious problems. He says the lack of honesty erodes intimate relationships and the fabric of community. Secrecy and deception are a toxic mix.

For many years I maintained a men's group in a church I formerly attended. I challenged the men to be forthcoming with others and led the way by sharing my own struggle with anxiety, my failures as a father and husband, and other secrets. I also told them about my defensiveness.

Although I found these years of "group therapy" to be arduous, they proved immensely healing. I discovered, as John Bradshaw also found, that attempts at speaking my truth—with only limited pretense and deception—was incredibly helpful. Meanwhile, the opposite approach—trying to manage others' perceptions of me through disguise and deception—was in no way beneficial. Pretense and deception were traits of crazy-makers that I no longer wanted in my life. Only by being forthcoming was I able to deal with them successfully.

I have concluded that except for certain special circumstances—such as when to do so would be harmful—total honesty is the best policy. This means not only telling the truth but also refraining from trying to manage others' perception of me by exaggerating personal strengths and minimizing personal weaknesses.

If someone wants to really know me, he or she must be strong enough to know my many foibles. Anything less erodes the integrity of our relationship.

Escaping the Net of Deception

Knowing that crazy-makers are dedicated to deception is a powerful insight, but it will be of little worth to you unless you use this knowledge to extricate yourself from their net. Consider how this can be done.

Get away from them. You cannot break free from the crazy-makers' distorted, confounding thinking patterns while standing in their presence. You must get away, even if you can only take small steps. Get away for an hour, then two, then four, then a day. You will not be able to sort things out while in the middle of the muddle. You need to get away. Consider going on a retreat or simply taking some time every day to determine exactly what is happening and why.

Be careful not to take what the crazy-makers say personally. Yes, this is very difficult to do, but you can do it. With enough emotional armor, you can avoid much of the sting of their harsh words. Dr. Albert Bernstein, in his book *Emotional Vampires,* offers the following counsel: "Use your confusion as a cue to stop and think about what's going on...Bullies' attacks are not personal. Bullies yell at everybody. If you think about it, the attacks actually say more about who and what Bullies are than they do about you."[7]

Seek verification of your truth. Nothing feels as good as having your perceptions validated. When you're in the middle of a crazy situation, nothing seems clear. We need trusted friends and confidants to tell us that what we are seeing is actually true.

Pray like crazy. Spend time alone with God, asking for His wisdom and guidance. God promises to give us wisdom in abundance if we will only ask for it. As we spend time alone with God, we begin to have the heart and mind of God.

Spend time in the Word. The psalmist says, "Delight yourself in the LORD and He will give you the desires of your heart" (Psalm 37:4). This verse states what is true of all believers who revel in their relationship with the Lord—their needs become their desires. What they desire for themselves matches God's desires for them.

Having spent time with your trusted friends and having prayed for guidance, rethink how you have been looking at the crazy-makers. With this fresh perspective you will be in a better position to decide what kind of relationship to have with them in the future. You are now much better prepared to determine how you choose to relate with them.

A Right to Privacy

Crazy-makers lack boundaries. They have a way of manipulating us into saying more than we are comfortable of saying and doing more than we want to do. We catch ourselves too late, after we've already spilled our guts. We must learn the importance of privacy.

Is laying our truth out there for everyone to see the only path to freedom? No. We will talk in future chapters about the critical need for boundaries. This issue can be complicated; some people in your life deserve to know the truth about you, but others are not entitled to such information.

I have revealed many intimate details of my life in my writings. You know that I have been divorced and, as much as I hate to say it, I was partially to blame for our marital demise. However, I will not share many of the intimate details about the breakup. They are not your business. It would be catty for me to reveal details about my ex—that is her personal business to share only if she chooses.

This is not deception. I am not attempting to manage your perception of me. It is enough for you to know that I have struggled with being a Christian, and a healer on top of that, and that even as a spiritual director I could not save my own marriage. It is enough for you to know that I contributed to the problems.

Deception is one thing. Privacy is quite a different matter, though not everyone will appreciate this distinction. Deception involves trying to manipulate your perception of me and events surrounding my life. Privacy is the setting of clear and honest boundaries. Let me further illustrate:

- I control access to a certain amount of emotional and physical space that I take to be mine.

- I protect myself from intrusion into those private areas.

- I guard against being the same as others by disagreeing or agreeing with certain people.

- I don't want my journal read, my mail opened, my office drawers rifled through, my phone tapped, or my values challenged without invitation.

- I don't want anyone entering my home without explicit agreement.

Dr. Harriet Lerner comments on this:

> I do not seek privacy in order to fool others or engage in acts of deception. Rather, I seek privacy primarily to protect my dignity and ultimate separateness as a human being. Thus, I publicly defend my "right to privacy." In contrast, I don't recall ever using the phrase, my "right to secrecy," although surely I have the right to keep some secrets, my own and others.[8]

It is important that we become clear about this issue—privacy doesn't mean secrecy. Secrecy involves withholding information that is appropriately shared, given the circumstances. Privacy involves withholding information that is appropriately private, thus serving ourselves and others better by keeping it so.

The Truth About Truth

The apostle John had much to say about truth. In addition to telling us that "the truth will set you free," he made some other bold statements that certainly have implications in dealing effectively with crazy-makers in our lives today.

> If we claim to have fellowship with him and yet walk in the darkness, we lie and do not live by the truth. But if we walk in the light, as he is in the light, we have fellowship with one another, and the blood of Jesus, his Son, purifies us from all sin (1 John 1:6-7).

John is saying that believers in Jesus Christ thirst for the truth. This is one of the hallmarks of Christians. Not content to believe in and live by the truth of this world, we seek another truth. We seek kingdom truth. We want to know what God thinks about particular matters.

Reading Scripture is a life-changing yet mind-boggling experience because much of what we learn in the world is antithetical to the ways of Jesus. The world tells us to take whatever steps are necessary to get what we want; Scripture tells us to lay down our life for a friend. The world says white lies can be useful in getting ahead; Scripture tells us, "Good people are guided by their honesty; treacherous people are destroyed by their dishonesty" (Proverbs 11:3 NLT).

The apostle John also wrote (forecasting end times), "Nothing evil will be allowed to enter—no one who practices shameful idolatry and dishonesty—but only those whose names are written in the Lamb's Book of Life" (Revelation 21:27 NLT).

Finally, John adds that if we walk in the light, we will enjoy fellowship with others. Is this not something we crave? In addition to our eternal reward of fellowship with Jesus, we also long for earthly relationships marked by peace.

As you allow yourself to be filled with light and truth, you will increase your opportunities for fellowship with others.

8

Foul Bait and Other Crazy-Making Lures

If your heart is a volcano,
how shall you expect flowers to bloom?

KAHLIL GIBRAN

My wife, Christie, worked in her grandfather's sports shop as a little girl. Kitsap Sports Shop, in downtown Bremerton, Washington, was a second home to avid fishermen, all looking for the latest lure that would help them reel in the next trophy fish.

Christie fondly recalls her grandfather, "Pops" Ray Stayner, opening a can of salmon eggs and pouring in anise extract. As if the salmon eggs were not enough to lure the fish, he found that this secret recipe enhanced the attraction of the bait. It also smelled up the store to high heaven.

She remembers the display cases of bright-colored spinners, lures, spoons, and rubber frogs and worms. There were all sizes of hooks, barbed and unbarbed, bobbers and sinkers, multicolored threads, and hand-tied flies—from dragonflies to mosquitoes.

Her attraction to lures and to fishing didn't end with childhood.

She developed a fascination that led her to collect old lures, fishing creels, and antique tackle boxes.

Lures and temptation have been part of our existence since the beginning of time. Consider the incident in the Garden of Eden. You recall that Adam and Eve were in their beautiful garden, which was filled with every possible delight. But they were forbidden to eat from one tree, and this tree contained something that appeared delicious and would reel them in.

We can imagine Adam and Eve sauntering through the garden, noticing a tempting tree loaded with ripe fruit. Though they knew this tree was off limits, Satan whispered that this fruit would make them like God—and who wouldn't want that? You know the rest of the story. Satan's temptation was the perfect complement for their desire, and they were hooked.

Crazy-makers use lures and bait to hook us. Employing their wiles, which seem to come naturally, they are able to catch us in their net of crazy-making behaviors. Some of their tactics seem well thought-out, deliberate strategies to get us into their boat. Others appear simply to be part of their character patterns. Either way, we often end up feeling paralyzed, stymied, befuddled, and crazy.

More Foul Bait

Having explored some of the ways we get hooked, in this chapter we will pay special attention to the thinking patterns of the members of the crazy-makers club. We will explore what experts have called "thinking errors" crazy-makers use, as well as why they might use them and their impact on us. We will learn how crazy-makers use these thinking styles to hook us, and examine how identifying these thinking styles can empower us to resist the bait.

In my counseling experience, I have found that most people are not aware of the thinking-error hooks crazy-makers use. Many people recognize that something is different about the way crazy-makers think, but they are unaware of exactly what it is.

The problem is that being unaware of these patterns leaves you vulnerable, unprepared to react in an effective and positive manner.

Being caught off guard by these antics can leave you paralyzed, unable to fight off the inevitable temptations. By applying the strategies discussed in this book to your particular situation, you will be able to shine a light on the hook, taking away much of its power to lure you into trouble.

Let's look at the broad array of "foul bait" crazy-makers use and the attraction this bait can wield. We'll consider which crazy-maker uses which particular types of thinking errors and discover strategies for dealing with each of them.

Over-Generalized Thinking

Over-generalized statements are exaggerations. You've heard them many times:

- You never listen to me.
- You always want your own way.
- Everybody expects too much of me.
- You should be doing things differently.

Statements like these have incredibly powerful hooks attached to them. They are barbed and dangerous. Let's consider why they are so hazardous and tempting.

Consider the power of an angry borderline's statements to her defenseless husband.

"You never listen to me. Whenever I try to talk to you, you turn away from me. I've told my friends about it, and they think you're neglecting me. You should be more loving, but you never are."

If you don't feel a bit confused after being subjected to an attack like that, you need to check your pulse. Imagine the husband's reaction as he is pelted by one generalization after another. We can easily imagine him responding angrily to his mate, stomping out of the room in disgust, or shrinking away in silence.

Most members of our company of crazy-makers exaggerate. Although this is more common to the aggressor, sufferer, and borderline, egotists and control freaks are quite capable of using over-generalized thinking as well.

How can a husband possibly respond to this bait, which a wife has designed specifically to vent her frustration?

First, of course, we must recognize the fallacy in her thinking. Knowing this information arms us with the ability to distance ourselves from the attack and actually choose how to respond instead of simply reacting negatively. Choosing the best way to respond is critical when faced with a powerful attack.

If we react, we're hooked. If we defend ourselves, we're hooked. So what are our options?

Over-generalized thinking is twisted, distorted, and terribly unfair. The best response is to simply acknowledge that you hear the person and sense her concern. As you have learned, if you try to defend yourself on each and every count, you'll be hopelessly hooked. Why? Because the accusations are vague, over-generalized, and quite possibly unfounded. To dive into them will leave you floundering on the sharp end of a hook.

Insisting that over-generalizers provide specific concerns can also be helpful. Tell them, "Please don't make generalizations. Tell me specifically what you need different from me." Make simple, powerful requests. This gets you unhooked because you are no longer buying everything they are saying about you and are putting the responsibility back on their shoulders.

Making Assumptions

Assumptions are another type of foul-smelling bait and often make us cringe with frustration. When people assume, they presume something is going to happen even though they have not laid out a clear argument that justifies it.

One of my patients, a sufferer, told me recently that she expected her husband to know that she wanted more time with him in the evenings. When I asked her if she had made these expectations clear, she looked surprised.

"Why should I have to tell him? He should know I need attention. We've been married ten years, but nothing's changed. I needed attention when we met, and I need it now. I assume he knows me well enough to figure it out on his own."

"How does he know exactly what kind of attention you want?"

"It shouldn't be that tough. He knows the way I'm wired, and he should be smart enough to respond accordingly."

"But I still don't understand how he's supposed to know exactly what you need."

"Like I told you, I shouldn't have to tell him things over and over. He knows what I need. He's just being stubborn and ignoring me."

Consider the assumptions that guide this woman's life and what she has to say to us.

- People should know exactly what I need. That's all there is to it.
- If they don't know what I need, they're just being stubborn.
- I am very important, and people should be dedicated to understanding and meeting my needs.
- If people don't recognize and fulfill my needs, they don't care about me.

These are the words and thinking patterns of a woman whose life is not working. She rarely gets her needs met because she doesn't make them clear to others. She doesn't think she should have to even though her current way of thinking does not work; in fact, it has never produced positive results.

The bait, and the accompanying hook in this case, is that we typically find out—through the crazy-makers' anger and exasperation—that we have failed them. Not wanting to do anything less than our best for a person we love, we try to read their minds. Of course, this is futile. We eventually give up, and then we are punished for doing so.

What to do?

Insist gently that assumers make their needs and expectations known. Repeat as often as necessary, "I can't read your mind. You'll have to tell me what you expect. Please don't assume something without checking it out with me. I want to make sure I understand."

Will assumers automatically give up their lifelong pattern of being passive-aggressive? Perhaps not immediately, but if their thinking and behavior pattern no longer hooks you, they just might try something more effective.

Mind Reading

You may be acquainted with mind reading. Here is an exchange I had with an aggressor who came with his wife to see me for marriage counseling.

Karl and Janice have been married for 25 years, none of them very happy. Karl, who is the manager of an auto parts supply store, reluctantly agreed to come to counseling with Janice. He came only because Janice was tired of his angry outbursts.

In the initial interview, I asked both why they had come for counseling. Janice offered her side of the story.

"I'm tired of Karl's temper. The least little thing sets him off, and I never know how he's going to react. If I leave the television on when I leave the house, he gives me a lecture. If I forget to put something back in the fridge, he'll stomp and mutter. I've had enough."

I turned to Karl and waited for his response.

"She deliberately tries to make me mad," he said. "She could turn off the TV, but she's too lazy. She doesn't think about my feelings. It's ironic because she's selfish, but she claims that I'm the selfish one. If I give her a lecture now and then, it's because she deserves it."

"Are you sure about those things, Karl? It seems like you're trying to read her mind. I think it would be better if you checked things out with her."

"I know how she thinks," he said emphatically. "I've lived with her for more than twenty years."

"Well," I said, "you may believe you know what she's thinking. But you don't really. It will relieve a lot of tension in your relationship if you made it clear that these are your perceptions and opinions, not hers."

"I can tell you what she's thinking," he insisted. "I know her."

Karl's mind reading can easily hook Janice if she isn't careful. She will need to repeatedly inform her husband that she does not want him to tell her what she is thinking. She might say something like this:

"Karl, please don't tell me what I'm thinking or imply that you know why I do things. And I would especially appreciate it if you didn't suggest that I have negative motives for my actions."

Janice will need to practice setting these boundaries with Karl. He may learn the first time, but he will more likely take time to discontinue his destructive habits.

Black-and-White and Either-Or Thinking

One of the control freak's favorite thinking errors is black-and-white, either-or thinking. Either he is for you, or he is against you. Either she agrees with you, or she doesn't. There is no middle ground. The control freak loves to pin you into a corner, making you feel confused and crazy.

Cary, 63, is married to Tamara. They are strong Christians and have been married nearly 20 years. This is the second marriage for both. Tamara initiated counseling following a particularly challenging weekend during which Cary, according to Tamara, had been belligerent and intimidating.

"Tell me what happened," I said at our first session.

Cary didn't hesitate.

"She went out for lunch with one of her friends after we agreed we were going to spend the time together. It's not the first time she has broken a promise to spend time with me. I'm tired of it."

"That's not the way it is at all," Tamara said. "He paints things to be one way, when they really aren't that way at all. I'm not a promise breaker, for heaven's sake. Cary is being ridiculous."

"How can you say that?" Cary said. "Did we have an agreement, or didn't we? Were we going to go out for dinner, or weren't we? Did you spend two hours with your friend, or didn't you?"

"This was an unusual situation, and you know it. Nancy called me because she was having trouble with her daughter, and I wasn't going to abandon her. And besides, I didn't cancel. I called and left a message with you that I'd be an hour late. Why is that such a big deal?"

Obviously not soothed, Cary launched into another tirade.

"The big deal is that you broke your promise. It happens all the time. In my book, people either keep the promises they make, or they don't. It's that simple."

Tamara looked to me for help. "Do you see how it is with him?" she said. "I just wanted to help my friend. I left a message with him, but that isn't good enough. If I mess up even a little, I feel like a kid being lectured in the principal's office. I'm not sure I can live like this."

"When you've argued about this type of thing in the past, have you been able to come up with solutions that work for you?" I asked.

"The solutions work fine," Tamara said, "as long as they're his solutions. As long as I always remember to report in to him where I'm going, who I'm with, and exactly when I'll be home. I used to go along with everything Cary said, but I'm changing now, and he doesn't like it. I love Cary, and I want to work things out. But I'm sick of having him dictate everything."

"She's becoming very rebellious," Cary said. "She is no longer a godly, submissive wife. Tamara has lost the meaning of submission, and that means she's not a good Christian as far as I'm concerned."

"I don't think the issue here is keeping promises," I said. "Your wife seems like a very sensitive person who makes obvious efforts to please you while also trying to be a good friend. I don't think that's enough to label her a promise breaker."

"It is in my book," he said. "And the Bible is the only book that matters."

I continued to work with Cary and Tamara for several months. We made very little progress. Cary was a control freak and liberally employed thinking errors in his attempt to control Tamara.

Tamara made progress not defending herself to Cary and expressing her opinion in spite of his opposition. I wish I could tell you they resolved all their issues and are living happily ever after, but that's not the case. As of this writing Cary and Tamara are separated and are considering what to do about their future. They are talking about how to be considerate with one another while not losing their individuality in the process.

Minimization

Egotists often use minimization to reduce problems they may have or their culpability. The egotist loves to make molehills out of mountains, and when mountains of problems are present, this tendency can drive a mate crazy.

I recall a couple who came to see me several years ago. The situation was unusual because Darrin was quite willing to come in for counseling. Part of the reason was that he did not think counseling would require any change on his part.

In typical egotist fashion, Darrin initially expressed disinterest when his wife, Debra, suggested they needed counseling. He informed me during their first and only session that he saw no need for counseling. "But if it makes her happy, why not?" he said.

Darrin came to the session with a cocky attitude. Debra was friendly and did her best to express her concerns.

"My life has been very unpredictable in the past few years," she said. "Once or twice a week Darrin stays out late playing poker at the casino, and I don't see him until the next morning. It's not so much the time away that I resent. It's the hundreds of dollars he loses that we can't afford."

"I don't think it's hundreds," Darrin said. "It's usually more like twenty-five or so. She's not counting the times I win. I know when to stop."

Debra sighed. "Honey," she said, "you don't realize how much you lose. I know because I track what's missing from our account. It's more than you think."

"Instead of talking about the amount that Darrin is losing," I said, "let's focus on the impact this is having on your marriage."

"I don't see any impact," Darrin said. "I love Deb, and I don't think the situation is that big of a deal. But if she wants me to cut back a little, hey, I can work with that."

"But you've said that before," Debra said. "That's why we're here now. What we've been doing isn't working."

I met with Darrin and Debra only that one time. I suspect Darrin would have been willing to come back. With his cavalier attitude, he may have thought he'd counsel me before the whole thing was over.

Perhaps for a variety of reasons, Debra caved in to Darrin. When I suggested to both Darrin and Debra that their problems were serious and needing significant intervention, both became noticeably agitated. I wasn't shocked to see Darrin become concerned, but I was surprised when Debra began to rationalize his behavior.

Minimization, in their case, would undoubtedly create even more trouble for them in the days and months ahead. But neither appeared to be willing to make the necessary changes to free themselves from the chaos of Darrin's gambling addiction.

What should you do if you are in a relationship with a minimizer? Minimization is a form of denial, so minimizers may or may not realize what they are doing. The most important thing is to refrain from buying into their minimization, which is what Debra did initially.

You must be clear about the truth and hold to it, even if the minimizer never acknowledges his thinking error. "That is not the way I see it. I believe…and I'd like you to…."

Repeat as needed.

Holding a Grudge

Sufferers seem to take pleasure in reminding people of how they have been wronged. They seem to hold on tenaciously to grievances. All of us, at one time or another, have held a grudge for far too long. We have nursed our bad feelings toward someone, letting too much time pass before moving forward in the relationship. Sufferers, however, are even more capable of clinging to the past than the rest of us. They not only remember past hurts, they remind you of them constantly.

Unforgiveness in a relationship is like a cancer out of control. It is bitterness turned against another again and again. To be the recipient of unforgiveness is to endure an agonizing form of crazy-making. People who hold grudges are holding you hostage. You cannot do anything to make them forget the alleged wrong you have done to them. Sufferers occupy a very powerful position if you allow yourself to be held hostage.

This is where you can take the power back from the grudge holder. Although not an easy task, it is possible. You can, with practice, learn to say to the grudge holder, "I'd like you to stop bringing up my mistakes. If you continue to punish me with my past, I won't be able to spend time with you." Drastic measures for drastic conditions. Separating yourself from a friend is easier than from a spouse, but the same counsel applies. Let your mate know you will not keep answering the same old questions and will refuse to spend time discussing well-worn topics.

The Scriptures are replete with examples of our need to forgive others. The parable of the unmerciful servant is particularly poignant because it instructs us about the imperative of forgiveness.

In Matthew 18:21-35, we read about the king who had forgiven the debt of a servant who couldn't have repaid it in a hundred lifetimes. The king forgave simply because he was asked to. The ungrateful servant, on the other hand, turned around and demanded full and immediate payment from a friend who had borrowed a much, much smaller sum.

We would expect the servant who had been forgiven so much to release his friend from the smaller debt. The servant's demand for payment demonstrated his lack of gratitude for what the king had done for him, and that's what aroused the king's anger. As a result, the king ordered his servant punished until he repaid all he owed.

In this story the ungrateful servant is a class-A crazy-maker. He is not about to forgive a debt even though he has been forgiven much. How many crazy-makers demand payment from us, keeping us hooked into them with their unforgiveness? Because we need their forgiveness, we become hooked. We may be overly eager for their acceptance, tolerating their abuse when we need to stand firm and express our unhappiness with their behavior.

Blaming Others

Most of us know the feeling of having a bony finger of blame pointed at us and how small it can make us feel.

"It's your fault." This is a powerful arrow, flung with precision by crazy-makers, particularly borderlines and aggressors. Randi Kreger, in her book *Stop Walking on Eggshells,* agrees:

> Continual blame and criticism is another defense mechanism that some people with Borderline Personality Disorder, who act out, use as a survival tool. The fault-finding may be pure fantasy on the BP's part or it can be an exaggeration of real-life problems.[1]

We can easily see how this kind of behavior can make others crazy. Being in a relationship with someone who constantly blames you for things you have done and for things you have not done is exasperating. The line between reality and fantasy blurs as you get hooked into trying to explain and defend yourself.

I often hear the following comments from people involved in relationships with borderlines:

- It's all about you.
- I can't win.
- I'm always to blame.
- You're never at fault.
- I'm in a no-win situation.
- I can't please you no matter how hard I try.

You can feel their frustration. They're caught in a debilitating relationship with no easy way out. Because blamers refuse to take responsibility for their mistakes, they remain stuck in their dysfunctional behavior.

Borderlines may continue blaming, but you must remind yourself that their attacks are about them, not you. This is their way of dealing with their own inner pain and turmoil. Though never pleasant, their barbs need not hook you, provided you remain clear about that point.

You can also throw back the hook by saying, "I won't accept blame for this. I did nothing wrong, and I'm not going to talk about it anymore."

Will the crazy-maker stop blaming you? Maybe not right away, but you can make it clear that you will not participate in the blame game.

Blaming Self and Over-Personalization

Being in a relationship with someone who refuses to take responsibility for her actions is unbearably frustrating. But just as tiresome is being in a relationship with someone, often a sufferer, who continually puts herself down.

Taking everything personally is an inverse form of narcissism. Think about it. The sufferer is saying, "It's all about me. I'm the worst person alive. I've failed more than anyone else. No one will ever be able to forgive me because of the magnitude of my actions."

Sufferers are usually thin-skinned and feel every slight that happens to them. A relational bump on the arm becomes an emotional compound fracture. The sufferer who overreacts to every incident has a huge pool of pain hidden inside that has never been healed.

If you are still getting hooked into trying to make the sufferer happy and guilt free, you're in for a long haul. You must remember that she has an investment in being more insecure than others, more upset than others, more guilty than others, more easily wounded than others. This is her trademark, and she is not likely to relinquish it easily—certainly not as long as it gets her mileage.

Remember, she is choosing to blame and punish herself, and you should not spend your energy trying to talk her out of her feelings. It won't work.

Uniqueness

Everyone in our corral of crazy-makers uses the hook of uniqueness. All of them, in their unique way, find a way to be special, to be better than and different from others.

Aggressors feel entitled to everything. Why? Well, because they are special. They are above the law. They either don't make mistakes like others, or more likely, they don't feel they have to own up to or pay for their mistakes.

Egotists claim to know more than anyone else, with perhaps the exception of the control freak. Egotists see themselves as exceptional individuals. They are, as you remember, legends in their own minds. Because they are so very special and are entitled to anything and everything, they'll overlook your needs as they demand center stage.

Sufferers are unique because life is more difficult for them than for others. They have more problems, more heartaches, and suffer far more than others. You'll find that they require a lot of attention and energy. They are high maintenance—at least until you decide that you're not going to keep paying the premiums required to keep them satisfied.

The borderline doesn't necessarily think she is unique. Her life is so chaotic, irrational, and dysfunctional, however, that she demands more energy than a healthier individual. In many ways, the borderline really is unique, though this is certainly not a compliment.

Control freaks are unique because they believe they have a corner on the truth and are convinced that others should acknowledge their dogmatic way of doing things. Control freaks won't admit they are special, but they will insist that they are right. This often leaves you grappling with two unpleasant options: acknowledging that they are right and admitting that you are wrong, or fighting to prove that they are not right. Neither approach will work.

How can we respond to people who demand to be treated uniquely?

Don't fall for it!

Don't give them preferential treatment. Don't bow down to them, idolize them, or tiptoe around them. When people quit treating them as unique, they often are forced to give up their superior position.

Denial

Having worked with clients who are under a legal mandate to see me, I am familiar with people looking me straight in the eyes and telling me they haven't used substances for the past six months. They may have failed their last four blood tests, but that somehow doesn't matter. They still look at me and tell me someone must have made some kind of mistake.

"Those blood tests are unreliable," they say. "You can't trust them."

You probably have your own version of this story. Perhaps you are married to a rage-aholic who conveniently forgets how angry he was last night. Maybe you are married to a woman who overspends, but when you confront her she insists she's not spending as much as the checkbook seems to say!

All of these stories have one thing in common—denial.

Denial is not just a river in Egypt, as they say. It's a pattern of failing to own up to the severity of the problem. It's people lying to themselves so much, so often, that they believe what they are saying.

And denial is an unconscious process, as opposed to outright deception, which we discussed in the last chapter. It is an unconscious, ingrained pattern of avoiding the truth, and it can drive friends and family to drink.

What can we do for people who are caught red-handed and still insist they are not to blame? Not much, other than to point out the truth to them lovingly, firmly, and with conviction.

You must speak the truth in love and camp there. No browbeating, no yelling and screaming, no name-calling. Just the truth.

Playing the Victim

Our last thinking error hook is a particularly potent one. It is called "playing the victim," and all of our crazy-makers use it, though sufferers and aggressors use it the most. Both find ways of twisting reality so that they appear to be getting a raw deal. The aggressor will be more aggressive as he acts out his inner rage, and the sufferer implodes with her anger. She makes others miserable by disregarding their boundaries and whining, "Poor me."

Aggressors and sufferers are not true victims, of course. God has not singled them out to be treated more harshly than the rest of us. The aggressor is his own worst enemy, setting himself up to be rejected by others and to lose jobs, marriages, and money. The Sufferer sets herself up to be victimized because she is so draining. No one wants to listen to her complain. She could step up and make positive changes in her life, but she refuses to do so.

Those of us who are rescuers don't want others to think or feel like a victim. So when they start in on their it's-not-fair routine, we jump in when we should leave things alone. When they put a spin on things, we need to simply smile inwardly and know that they are trying to get us to acknowledge their painful plight and rescue them.

Don't fall for it.

As a Man Thinketh

You may have heard of James Allen. He is a literary mystery man whose inspirational writings have influenced millions of people. Still, surprisingly, he remains virtually unknown.

Allen wrote 19 books during the nineteenth century but never gained fame or fortune. He barely made enough money from his books to cover expenses. He evidently rose at dawn, climbed the hills surrounding his humble home in England to commune with God, and then spent the balance of the morning writing. He spent his afternoons gardening and conversing with friends. The title from his second book, *As a Man Thinketh,* comes from Proverbs 23:7. The book includes this passage:

> A man is literally what he thinks, his character being the complete sum of all his thoughts. As the plant springs from, and could not be without, the seed, so every act of man springs from the hidden seeds of thought, and could not have appeared without them…A noble character is not a thing of favor or chance, but is the natural result of continued effort in right thinking, the effect of long-cherished association with God-like thoughts.

Allen is considered one of the forerunners of modern-day psychology. He determined that if we think troubling and negative thoughts, we will have troubling behavior. If we change our thoughts, we can change our behavior.

Crazy-makers would do well to consider the importance of Allen's work. Because they have distorted perceptions, crazy-makers also have distorted and twisted behaviors. Allen would certainly subscribe to the notion that if you live with thinking errors, such as those described in this chapter, you will experience significant problems in your life.

As a man thinks, so is he.

Renewing Your Mind

James Allen was obviously inspired by the wisdom of Solomon. Solomon's words are later supported by the apostle Paul, who instructs us about our thinking:

> Do not conform any longer to the pattern of this world, but be transformed by the renewing of your mind. Then you will be able to test and approve what God's will is—his good, pleasing and perfect will (Romans 12:2).

Here is our hope for dealing with not only the thinking errors of crazy-makers but also the crazy-makers themselves. Each of us has the opportunity to renew our minds and then to test and approve God's will for our lives. This is powerful stuff. Let's take a closer look at the instruction given in this passage.

First, we are not to be conformed to the pattern of this world. What is the pattern of this world? In my counseling practice, I listen to a lot of self-centered, immature, grandiose thinking patterns. I see a lot of people demanding their own way and being insensitive to the needs of others. I hear a lot of distorted thinking that could be remedied by spiritual maturity. As Christians, we are to be set apart from these destructive thinking patterns. But how are we to do this when in our flesh we want our way?

Second, we are to be transformed by the renewing of our minds. There it is! The apostle Paul says that we are not to simply think differently, as important as that is, but to have *renewed* minds. That means that we must have new minds. The apostle Paul says it again in his letter to the Ephesians:

> You were taught, with regard to your former way of life, to put off your old self, which is being corrupted by its deceitful desires; to be made new in the attitude of your

minds; and to put on the new self, created to be like God
in true righteousness and holiness (Ephesians 4:22-24).

Paul has much to say about mind control and the devastation
that occurs when we live according to desires of the flesh. He must
have known something about crazy-makers.

Those who live according to the sinful nature have
their minds set on what that nature desires; but those
who live in accordance with the Spirit have their minds
set on what the Spirit desires. The mind of the sinful man
is death, but the mind controlled by the Spirit is life and
peace (Romans 8:5-6).

Paul's words are incredibly hopeful. In the flesh, according to our
natural desires, we will struggle against "the pattern of this world."
That means we will not only battle the thinking errors of crazy-makers
but also possess some of those same traits ourselves. However, when
we walk in the Spirit, our minds are transformed. We experience a
metamorphosis.

Like the caterpillar turning into the butterfly, our minds change
from the inside out. Instead of gritting our teeth and desperately
trying to change, we experience change naturally when we submit
to the Spirit of God. Don't settle for a patch job. Seek instead a renewed mind. When you are tempted by the crazy-makers' thinking
patterns, offer your mind as a living sacrifice, available for renewal,
holy and pleasing to God.

In our next chapter, the final chapter of this section on the ways
we get hooked by crazy-makers, we will explore patterns of interaction that you can change to avoid being reeled in. A little knowledge
equals a lot of constructive power!

9

The Powerful Bait
of Irresponsibility

He who does a good deed is instantly ennobled.

RALPH WALDO EMERSON

"I'm not going to raise another child!" Sandi screamed as she jumped out of her chair and headed for my office door. When she reached the door she paused, turned around and put her hands on her hips. Her husband Tom and I sat motionless, wondering what was coming next.

"I am so tired of having to be the responsible one in this marriage," she said. "You can decide what you want to do, but I am not playing this game any longer. I needed your help with the kids for twenty years and never got it. I need you to pick up after yourself. I need you to quit taking money out of the checking account without telling me. I need you to keep your promises. But you haven't been able to do even one of those things, and now I'm done."

Sandi slammed the door, rattling the window above my desk. We heard her footsteps as she stomped down the stairs.

I had been seeing Tom and Sandi only a few weeks but had already learned that responsibility, or rather a lack of responsibility, was a serious threat to their marriage. I knew Sandi had reached her limit with her responsibilities and desperately needed Tom to pick up the pace.

"I don't know why she's like that," Tom said. "I hate being treated like a child." He gripped his chair and scowled.

"I can see why it would bother you," I said. "Sandi is very angry, that's for sure. Let's put our heads together and try to figure out how much of her anger belongs to you, and what part of it is hers. Okay?"

"All right. But I can't see anyone getting that mad over a pair of work boots left out in the middle of the kitchen floor. It definitely wasn't enough to justify that kind of explosion."

"I don't think Sandi is just angry about you leaving your work boots in the middle of the kitchen floor. As I recall, we've been talking about a number of issues like this one. Wasn't she angry a few weeks ago when you didn't pick the kids up from school like you promised? And before that, didn't you refuse to help keep the house clean because you felt that working long hours at the mill ought to be enough?"

"Sandi is always mad about something. If it wasn't my work boots, she'd be complaining about how much time I spend with the kids. And if not that, then about how I spend money. I can't win, and I'm just as tired of it as she is."

"You need to keep in mind that in each of these instances you made promises that you didn't keep," I said. "Each time, you apologized later for not holding up your end of the bargain and for your angry response when she called you on it."

Tom looked up at me and seemed to soften.

"Maybe you guys are right," he said. "I don't know why I keep breaking promises, but I do. I guess I can see why she gets mad, but it still seems like an overreaction to me."

Tom's interaction with Sandi reminded me of my interaction with my father many years ago. My dad insisted I abide by the curfew we had agreed upon. Caught up in staying out with my friends, I pushed the limits repeatedly. And he got angry repeatedly. Our interactions went something like this:

"David, why do you keep coming in late when we've agreed on a set time?"

"It wasn't a big deal. I just got caught up in what I was doing. Besides, I wasn't that late. It won't happen again."

"You've told me that over and over. I can't trust you anymore. I make agreements with you, and you break them."

"There you go again," I would say hotly. "You're always accusing me of not being able to be trusted. I said that I won't let it happen again. What more do you want from me?"

"We've had this talk time and again, but your behavior never changes. I don't know what to do anymore."

And so it would go. My father would scold me for my irresponsibility, and I would get angry with him for scolding me. It was a dysfunctional, crazy-making conversation with no apparent way out. Like Tom and Sandi, we were engaged in a power struggle over responsibility—another major issue with the crazy-maker.

Disorders of Responsibility

We've talked about crazy-makers and the tactics they use to hook us. In the last few chapters, we discussed their tendency to use deception as a hook, as well as the thinking errors they employ to drive us batty. In this chapter, we will look through the lens of responsibility to examine how crazy-makers view the world and ultimately hook us.

Crazy-makers are often incredibly careless, and we are expected to pick up the pieces left in their wake. But when we do, we get hooked by becoming overly responsible. Fortunately, we can take steps to encourage responsibility in crazy-makers while making sure we don't take their bait.

Scott Peck offers a helpful way of thinking about this issue. He says people come to see psychiatrists for two reasons: They are struggling with either a character disorder or neurosis.

> These conditions are disorders of responsibility, and as such are opposite styles of relating to the world and its problems. The neurotic assumes too much responsibility;

the person with the character disorder, not enough. When neurotics are in conflict with the world they automatically assume that they are at fault. When those with character disorders are in conflict with the world they automatically assume that the world is at fault.[1]

Peck was one of the first to put this information into language that lay people could understand. Listen to what he says about crazy-makers and the problems they have with responsibility.

> Those with character disorders [most of our crazy-makers!] are much more difficult, if not impossible, to work with because they don't see themselves as the source of their problems; they see the world, rather than themselves as being in need of change and therefore fail to recognize the necessity of self-examination.[2]

Peck goes on to explain that many people actually have a combination of neurotic and character disorders, some tending to take too much responsibility and some too little. Some live in guilt because they have assumed responsibility that is not really theirs. However, most of the crazy-makers we've examined in this book fail to take responsibility for their lives. The task, Peck says, is to engage people in examining and correcting their unwillingness to assume responsibility where appropriate.

Sandi was weary of confronting Tom about his negligence. Tom had glimmers of insight similar to the one he exhibited in my office, yet he repeatedly fell back into irresponsible behavior. He did so because he ultimately wanted to make the problem Sandi's. If she, as he alleged, was simply too critical, why should he be expected to change?

If she was never going to be satisfied, as he insisted was the case, why even try? Why go through the painful efforts of self-examination and character adjustment if she was simply going to move the target? So Tom made changes very, very reluctantly, if at all.

My father confronted my irresponsibility by scolding and lecturing me, trying to get me to see the error of my ways. It did not work. In fact, his lecturing was not backed up with firmer action, so it only enabled my irresponsibility.

For years I was able to deceive and convince myself that he was simply an angry man who had it out for me. Playing the victim, I escaped responsibility—though ultimately this was not helpful to my character development. Seeing him as the bad guy, I rebelled and lived life on my own terms.

Not surprisingly, my adolescent years were very difficult. Not only was I enraged at my father, but I danced on the edge of trouble with the law as well, driving recklessly, narrowly escaping serious injury on two occasions. I allowed my grades to suffer and was perilously close to not graduating from high school because I chose to live life my way.

I viewed the world through my own selfish lens, often becoming angry when that world did not conform to my expectations. I saw my parents, the law, and authority figures in general as being out to get me. I was unwilling to admit that I was causing my own problems. The world according to David could easily have led to self-destruction.

Fortunately, perhaps more by God's grace than my own doing, I ended up at Covenant Bible College in Prince Albert, Saskatchewan, after graduating from high school. However, my behavior didn't change. I again tested limits and assumed I didn't have to be responsible. I failed classes and refused to take the dorm restrictions seriously. I was nineteen years old going on nine—and driving everyone around me crazy with my irresponsibility.

I believed rules were meant to be broken—at least until I ended up in the office of the president of the school. In a frank discussion with Reverend Anderson, I learned that either my misbehavior would cease or I would be expelled. He wanted me to succeed, but he had no qualms about sending me home. He and the school were committed to integrity and respect for the rules. The choice was mine.

This was an epiphany for me. My life was not working. I still dreamed of being the CEO and CFO of the world according to David, but I decided the time had come to call for assistance. My business was failing. Angry, sullen, and distraught, I finally chose to look in the mirror. Enough blaming others in an attempt to escape responsibility.

The thought of being expelled from school and returning home in disgrace did not appeal to me. At long last, I began the process of taking responsibility for my behavior and my life. This was the beginning of a wonderful healing experience with my parents, especially my dad.

Irresponsibility and Disrespect

It is one thing to implode, as I was doing during my adolescence and early adulthood. We can destroy our own lives and get away with it because we hurt mainly ourselves. Unfortunately, irresponsibility usually results in the destruction of others' lives as well.

Reverend Anderson told me clearly and dispassionately that I was free to ruin my life. However, I would not be allowed to stay on his campus and taint the reputation of the school. My father should have said the same thing to me earlier—I was free to disregard the rules of my own life but not those that affected the family.

Our group of crazy-makers has responsibility disorders that impact others. They are generally unwilling to do the hard work of facing their issues and determining what things they are and are not responsible for. They do not, without significant intervention, have the capacity or willingness to suffer self-examination, reviewing where they fail to take responsibility. They are more content to take the easy path of blaming others, minimizing their own actions, and denying culpability.

Consider Sandi's life. She stormed out of our session because she was tired of raising another child. What she learned to say to Tom over the following weeks in counseling was this: "Tom, you are free to disregard things that affect only your life. But when you repeatedly create problems for me and our children, that's where I draw the line."

Crazy-makers who avoid responsibility ultimately have a problem with respecting others. They live selfish lives, focused on pleasing themselves in spite of the effect on those around them. In addition, crazy-makers are unaware that disrespect works both ways. When we recognize crazy-makers' hooks, we lose respect for them.

Gerald May refers to this in his bestselling book *Addiction and Grace:*

> We are part of larger systems whether we want to be or not, and if our journey is consecrated we must recognize our responsibility for participating in the lovingness of those systems. At its simplest level, responsibility means respecting ourselves and those around us. In the nature of systems, all our addictive behaviors affect other people. Some behaviors really hurt others. We have a responsibility to try to identify and restrain those behaviors. In practical terms, we must listen to what other people are telling us, notice what effects we are having on them, and be willing to change.[3]

May's words are worthy of closer scrutiny. Keeping our group of crazy-makers in mind, consider how they fare at these tasks.

Respect ourselves and those around us. Certainly we agree that the aggressor does not respect himself or others when he blows up and resorts to intimidating those who disagree with him. To take advantage of others, to manipulate them for personal gain, is disrespectful.

Identify and restrain irresponsible behaviors. To fail to identify and eliminate troubling behaviors is disrespectful. For the borderline to rage, to demand things go her way, and to twist the truth to make herself appear virtuous are all disrespectful.

Listen to what others are telling us. When egotists act pompous and self-righteous, insisting that their way of doing things is the only way, when they are so caught up in their own agendas that they simply refuse to listen to your point of view, they are being disrespectful.

Notice the effect our behavior has on others. When sufferers won't stop to notice the impact of their whining about how wronged they have been, when they fail to acknowledge the harm caused by their attempts to triangulate and hook you with their emotions, they are being disrespectful.

Be willing to change. Control freaks resist change. Regardless of how often you confront them, they seem to persist with their point of view. When control freaks insist on having their way, you are diminished and made to feel smaller. This is disrespectful.

Power in Naming Disrespect

Labeling the crazy-makers' hooks as troubling is one thing; labeling them as irresponsible and disrespectful can be empowering. When I recognize my patterns of deception and self-centeredness as irresponsible, I squirm with discomfort. When I admit that my actions are disrespectful, I want to crawl under a rock.

When I was growing up, I thought my actions affected only me—very short-sighted thinking on my part. By identifying my behavior as disrespectful, I admitted that I was treating my family with disrespect. This caused me to reconsider whether I really wanted to continue with my self-centered approach to life.

Sandi's storming out of my office clearly signaled a high level of distress. She was not just upset. She was nearing the point of no return. Tom's failure to keep agreements, to abide by agreements they had made in the past, had created profound disrespect. As a result, Sandi was seriously considering whether she wanted to remain married to a man who would treat her this way.

Sandi had sabotaged herself many times with self-doubt. She had wondered if she was overreacting to Tom's lack of responsibility. How could leaving a pair of boots on the kitchen floor cause such distress? Why did his refusal to do part of the housecleaning cause her such anger? The answer is that a part of her recognized his actions as profoundly disrespectful. When Tom exploded after being confronted about his violations, this only added insult to Sandi's injuries.

John Gottman, in his landmark book *Why Marriages Succeed or Fail*, identifies predictable signs that indicate whether a marriage will succeed or fail. One of the signs of impending failure is contempt, which is a product of disrespectful behavior that continues over a long period of time. Gottman shares the following story, which is strikingly similar to my experience with Sandi and Tom.

> By their first anniversary, Eric and Pamela still hadn't resolved their financial differences. Unfortunately, their

fights were becoming more frequent and more personal. Pamela was feeling disgusted with Eric. In the heat of one particular nasty argument, she found herself shrieking, "Why are you always so irresponsible? You never pay attention to how much you spend. You're so selfish." Fed up and insulted, Eric retorted, "Oh shut up. You're just a stingy cheapskate who doesn't know how to live. I don't know how I ended up with you anyway." The second horseman—contempt—had entered the scene.[4]

I don't know anything about Eric and Pamela aside from this excerpt from Gottman's book. But their marriage is clearly in serious trouble. I know this as surely I know that Sandi and Tom's marriage is in serious trouble. I know this because Sandi stormed out of my office, because she is tired of Tom's irresponsibility, because Tom wants to blame her outbursts on high standards and impossible expectations.

Gottman tells us that we must take contempt very seriously because it is so often the result of chronic irresponsibility and a failure to resolve it. Left unchecked, irresponsibility leads to chronic disrespect, which leads to contempt, which ultimately leads to the dissolution of a relationship.

The Power of Disrespect

The crazy-makers in your life probably don't understand the power of their irresponsibility. It is, after all, an ingrained part of who they are. It is as natural to them as breathing. They also may not realize the damage their irresponsibility can cause to a relationship. If they are ever to become aware of the harm they are causing, you will need to take the first step in alerting them to the situation. Dr. Albert Bernstein, in his book *Emotional Vampires,* explains the power of disrespect on a relationship.

> Night-stalking vampires will drain your blood. Emotional Vampires will use you to meet whatever needs they happen to be experiencing at the moment. They have no

qualms about taking your effort, your money, your love, your attention, your admiration, your body, or your soul to meet their insatiable cravings. They want what they want, and they don't much care how you feel about it.[5]

Take a moment to assess how you feel when reading these words. "They will use you to meet whatever needs they happen to be experiencing at the moment."

Does this mean that crazy-makers don't care about you? Not necessarily. Are they driven by their own immediate needs? Most certainly—and by their deceptive thinking errors, which can ultimately hook the people around them. Bernstein says that our band of crazy-makers is generally driven by these irresponsible beliefs:

- My needs are more important than yours.
- The rules apply to other people, not to me.
- It's not my fault—ever.
- I want it now.
- If I don't get my way, I'll throw a tantrum.

No wonder your relationship suffers when your mate is so self-centered that he has no respect for others and places his needs before anyone else's. Are you really surprised when you begin to lose respect for the crazy-maker? Being constantly angry and annoyed with him makes perfect sense. Losing your love for him is logical.

For crazy-makers to be unaware of their actions and continue them anyway is one thing. For us to enable these destructive processes is quite another. We ignorantly enable egotists to blast their way into our lives and push their own agenda. We are overwhelmed by the rage of the aggressors and the emotionality of the borderlines, thereby enabling their behavior. We have mixed feelings for sufferers that often prevent us from confronting them. We feel subjugated by the argumentativeness of control freaks.

But what are we to feel if we have confronted our mate about such behavior and the violations continue month after month, year after year?

The answer is clear—we develop a profound disrespect for them and sometimes a similar level of disrespect for ourselves. A deep and tragic pain often unfolds, leading to the demise of the relationship.

When irresponsibility erodes respect, the erosion of love cannot be far behind.

Caring Equals Responsible Action

If irresponsibility and inaction erode love and respect, we can rebuild love and respect with responsible action—what Sam Keen refers to as "caring." In his book *To Love and Be Loved,* Keen says caring involves skillful concern.

> Our feelings of generosity and our desire to care do not automatically translate into wisdom. A large part of the practice of love involves knowing what to give to whom…A gift may be an instrument of grace that empowers its recipient or a disguised weapon that cripples. Questionable motives may trigger seemingly care-ful acts.[6]

I still feel ashamed about the way I treated my parents during my adolescence. I was not caring or careful with my family. I was raised in nearly idyllic circumstances. My parents treated me with special compassion and attention. I have many rich memories of being nurtured in a family of love.

I remember having many neighborhood friends at my house when I was a child. They knew that my parents welcomed and accepted them. I recall numerous innocent escapades with my neighborhood chums, Kenny, Donald, Mike, and Danny. I grew up in the Swedish Evangelical Covenant Church, where I received a vibrant heritage of faith.

I remember my mother and father's doting attention and care. On one occasion, when I was a young teenager, my father drove me to my junior high school and took a teacher to task for some transgression against me (I don't recall the issue). What stays with me is my father's fierce protectiveness, which exists to this day. My father and mother care for me and attend to me still. They embodied what Keen describes:

> Care moves love from feeling into action, from self
> to other, from getting to giving. When we care, we take
> responsibility for and seek the well-being and fulfillment
> of another person; our capacity for empathy, compassion,
> and sympathetic enjoyment is mobilized on behalf of a
> child, a friend, a lover, a stranger in distress.[7]

This says it all. When people really care for us, they demonstrate it. They show us by being responsible in their actions. They go out of their way to protect us, to know us, to make sure we feel their attentive actions.

No wonder Sandi winces in pain at Tom's inaction and irresponsibility. He says, "I love you," and then disregards the very thing she has asked for as a sign of his caring. He says, "I love you," and then forgets the important agreement they made hours earlier. His words become a sham. They lose their sincerity and meaning.

Keen does not shrink from raising a difficult question: Are we asking others to forsake themselves so we can meet our needs? Keen encourages us to care for ourselves and for others:

> If I neglect the cultivation of my gifts, the nurturing of
> my deepest needs, the enjoyment of those pleasures that
> tickle my peculiar fancy, it is unlikely that my caring for
> others will spring from the bounty of my being. Whenever
> we abandon our personal sense of vocation and joie de
> vivre, we place an enormous burden on others to justify
> the sacrifices we have made for "for their sake"...Develop
> those modes of caring that allow you to love both self and
> others. The sacrifices love demands of us should make our
> lives rich in meaning and satisfaction.[8]

A Time for Tough Love

The crazy-makers' irresponsibility may eventually become overwhelmingly exhausting. When you feel "baited" one time too many, you're finally ready for action.

Sandi was at that point when she stormed out of my office. She was so ready that she called me an hour later, saying she was prepared for "tough love." We discussed what that might look like and the implications it might have for her and the children.

Together we agreed that she would write a letter to Tom and let him consider the implications. Here is her letter:

> Dear Tom,
>
> I have always been committed to you and to our marriage. However, your constant neglect in keeping agreements has caused me to lose respect for you. You repeatedly make promises but don't follow through with them. You minimize the impact of your irresponsibility on me, and that is infuriating. I can no longer live like this. I am going to spend a few days away from you, maybe longer. I want you to consider your actions and decide if you are willing to keep the agreements we have made in counseling. I don't like the person I'm becoming—always angry with you for your irresponsibility. I will meet you in our counseling session next week, and we can talk more about this issue. I love you and look forward to a lifetime together once we have resolved this situation.
>
> Love, Sandi

Sandi decided she would no longer tolerate or enable her husband's irresponsible behavior. She wanted to respect Tom, but she needed him to keep his agreements in order for her to do so. Tom, as it turned out, had resentment of his own that he was expressing by being passive-aggressive. He didn't really agree with the promises he was making, so he sabotaged them. Through talking about this in counseling, he learned to disagree with Sandi when appropriate. Conversely, when he made agreements, he determined that he would keep them. But only drastic measures got him to that point.

Gary Chapman includes this comment in his book *Loving Solutions*:

> If we are to be constructive change agents toward irresponsible spouses, we must always consider what motivates their irresponsible behavior, what is going on inside the individual. Unless we are able to address these issues, we are not likely to see positive change.[9]

Chapman goes on to advocate tough love for chronically irresponsible spouses, which can include separation if they do not change.

Emotional Overfunctioning

I am indebted to Dr. Harriet Lerner for her pioneering work with women and especially to the crazy-makers' use of irresponsibility. However, Lerner doesn't stop at challenging the irresponsible spouse. She understands that Ms. Responsibility often links up with Mr. Irresponsibility, subconsciously believing this may be a match made in heaven. Lerner nudges women to inspect their motives and behaviors and to consider if they have created the very dynamics that drive them crazy. She encourages women to critically inspect their lives to see if they have taken on the role of "overfunctioner."

> Often in relationships, women overfunction by assuming a "rescuing" or "fix-it" position. We behave as if it is our responsibility to shape up other people or solve their problems, and further, that it is in our power to do so. We may become reactive to every move that a person makes or fails to make, our emotions ranging from annoyance to intense anger and despair. And when we realize our attempts to be helpful are not working, do we stop and do something different? Of course not...
>
> But what is wrong with taking responsibility for others? In some respects, nothing. For generations, women have gained both identity and esteem from our deep investment in protecting, helping, and nurturing, and comforting others...The problem arises when we are excessively reactive to other people's problems, when we assume responsibility for things that we are not responsible for, and when we attempt to control things that are not in our control.[10]

Sandi's situation may be more complex than it appears. The tentacles of responsibility run deep in her relationship. She may wish Tom were more responsible, but allowing him to actually grow in responsibility may be more challenging than she imagines. For a long time, he has under-functioned while she has over-functioned. She must relinquish responsibility for him becoming more accountable in their home and marriage.

Striving for Maturity

We cannot talk about letting go of crazy-making irresponsibility and growing into caring responsibility without discussing spiritual maturity. We are spiritual beings, and our behavior and emotions are not separate from the role that faith plays in our lives. One could argue that we cannot become emotionally mature, gaining the ability to truly care for others, without possessing spiritual maturity. Certainly being mature spiritually assists us in the path of emotional maturity, and being a crazy-maker is inconsistent with the Christian faith.

The Scriptures highlight the importance of being responsible and spiritually mature. In fact, one of the apostle Paul's central messages was that we should become mature and responsible Christians. He makes clear that the pure and healthy love that accompanies maturity and responsibility is antithetical to crazy-making.

> And this is my prayer: that your love may abound more and more in knowledge and depth of insight, so that you may be able to discern what is best and may be pure and blameless until the day of Christ, filled with the fruit of righteousness that comes through Jesus Christ—to the glory and praise of God (Philippians 1:9-11).

Paul didn't expect people to gain instant maturity once they accepted Christ. He knew full well that maturation is a process.

> Not that I have already attained all this, or have already been made perfect, I press on to take hold of that for which Christ Jesus took hold of me. Brothers, I do not consider myself yet to have taken hold of it...All of us who are mature should take such a view of things (Philippians 3:12-13,15).

What are some indicators of spiritual maturity? In the passage above, Paul notes that sacrificial love will abound among those who are mature. He goes on to say that they will be able to discern what is best and pure. With that power, they will be filled with the fruit of righteousness, which will enable them to pursue the ways of God.

Followers of Christ who strive for spiritual maturity will be marked by two key traits. First, they will surrender their own desires to the desires of God. No longer serving the master of self, they serve God. Second Timothy 2:15 tells us, "Do your best to present yourself to God as one approved, a workman who does not need to be ashamed and who correctly handles the word of truth." The crazy-maker who dedicates his life to God will eventually mature.

Second, Christians who strive for spiritual maturity will be obedient to God and to His Word. They will read the Word of God and seek to apply its principles to their lives. Because the Word of God changes lives, maturity is a natural byproduct. "All scripture is God-breathed and is useful for teaching, rebuking, correcting and training in righteousness, so that the man of God may be thoroughly equipped for every good work" (2 Timothy 3:16).

Spiritual maturity, if it is genuine, will have an impact on responsibility and emotional maturity. Those who follow after God and seek His ways, which include loving others, will increasingly strive to change their way of thinking. No longer conforming to the standards of this world, they will become less self-centered, more giving, less judgmental, and increasingly tolerant of others. Spiritual maturity will have a remarkable ability to transform our relationships. The old self will fade and the new self will emerge.

Crazy-makers can benefit from this one critical antidote: dedicating their lives to being filled with the love of Christ and watching their thinking and life change dramatically as spiritual maturity leads them to a higher path.

> Love is patient, love is kind. It does not envy, it does
> not boast, it is not proud. It is not rude, it is not self-seeking
> (1 Corinthians 13:4-5).

PART THREE

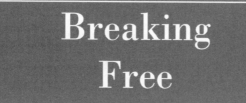

Breaking
Free

10

Boundaries Deliver Freedom

For one human being to love another, that is the work
for which all other work is but preparation.

RAINER MARIA RILKE

After an incredibly long winter, spring has finally arrived. My wife and I are busy unpacking boxes and moving into a new place of our own. Our home is perched on a bluff overlooking beautiful Hood Canal, tucked neatly onto the northwest tip of Washington State. I feel as if I can see forever. The peaks of the Olympic Mountains, which are usually snow-capped, are now dappled with gray. The morning sunlight shimmers across the water, and sailboats propelled by the gusty wind skitter past.

Skiffs huddle around tiny bobbing flags that mark the location of crab pots. The crabs don't stand much of a chance. Lured by chicken bait, they will instinctually seek food and enter a swing gate to reach their meal. Once the gate swings closed, they're trapped, and someone will soon be enjoying fresh Dungeness crab for dinner.

A similar scene is replayed many times every day, not only in the fishing and crabbing industry—which features the trap, the lure, the bait, and the catch—but in our lives as well. Unsuspecting people

167

rise to crazy-makers' bait and are hooked into a life of frustration and dysfunction.

This book is attempting to change that, and in this section we will focus on what you can do to break free from the trap you are now in and develop life patterns that will help you avoid being hooked in the future.

Can you imagine a life that is not dictated by the crazy-makers? Rather than ambling along unsuspectingly one moment and finding ourselves emotionally trapped the next, let's work together to establish strategies that will keep you free.

Enabling the Crazy-Maker

We ended the last chapter with a brief discussion about how we unconsciously enable the crazy-maker with our own over-functioning. We now need to take a closer look at this issue. When we can change our patterns, we will help them change theirs.

Do you believe that one person can change a dysfunctional family pattern? It's true. The family system relies on every person fulfilling his or her particular role, so when one person changes the pattern, the whole system changes.

Picture a mobile with six or seven pieces hanging from the ceiling of your house. Take one piece and shake it. Every other piece in the mobile is affected. Most of the time we think of this from a negative vantage point: The crazy-maker walks into the house, hooks us into his nutty behavior, and the entire family suffers. Yes, one crazy-maker can rattle an entire household. But the opposite is also true—one healthy person can put a family on the path to positive interaction.

Jesus understood the impact that one person could have on an entire system. He said, "Be on your guard against the yeast of the Pharisees and Sadducees" (Matthew 16:11). A little bit of their false teaching could contaminate an entire body of believers. The leavening process of deception could work its way into the thinking and behavior of the entire church.

He also taught us that the right ingredient can have a broad, positive influence. "The kingdom of heaven is like yeast that a woman took and mixed into a large amount of flour until it worked all through the dough" (Matthew 13:33). The kingdom of heaven can be penetrating and life-changing. It can transform single lives and entire communities and nations. One person—you—can make a difference.

To make a difference, however, we must first understand how we enable crazy-makers to worm their way into our lives and wreak havoc. Let's review some of the flawed behaviors that open the door to crazy-makers, and then we'll discuss strategies to break free from these errors.

Accepting or making excuses. Yes, in spite of the exasperating behavior of crazy-makers, we are tempted to accept their excuses. They don't understand what you mean when you refer to their demanding attitude or constant complaining. They appear to have no awareness of their aggressive behavior or the way they twist your words. You wonder if they can possibly "get it," but you tell yourself they may just need more time, effort, or faith to get there. Perhaps you decide to talk to them again, explaining that their behavior is troubling. Maybe for the briefest moment they seem to understand. But not long after, they repeat their damaging behavior again.

In exasperation, you find yourself talking too loudly, explaining too much, making too many excuses for their crazy-making behavior. You want to calm down the situation. The myriad of excuses continues, all to avoid the pain of telling it like it is. They must be held accountable for their crazy-making behavior, and this will be uncomfortable for them and for you. They *can* change, especially if no one is enabling their dysfunctional behavior.

Justifying behavior. Yes, they are responsible for their actions, you say, but they've had a rough life. You understand their crazy-making and attempt to rationalize it. You put it in the larger context of their upbringing, their hard work life, their temperament. And the list goes on. Holding crazy-makers accountable may create even more problems in the short run, so you justify their behavior so they no longer have to change.

"He works hard and can be irritable on night shift."

"She's been alone her whole life. She can't help being a martyr at times."

"He's full of himself, but he's a lot of fun too."

Picking up the pieces. Yes, ladies, I'm talking to you now. How often have you bailed him out of a jam just because you could? As Harriet Lerner says, you've learned to over-function. When he "forgets" to take care of business, you're right there to step in. When he is absorbed in his own activities and can't seem to be bothered by family responsibilities, you pick up the kids, get them fed, and manage the home in his absence. You are over-responsible in response to his under-responsibility—all the while enabling his crazy-making behavior to continue.

Ignoring problems. As much as the crazy-maker uses denial to avoid the problem, you may be guilty of turning your head. You may have chosen not to see the problem. You're as surprised as anyone when a friend asks you why you put up with these crazy-making ways. Their words jolt you back to reality—that's right, you're married to a control freak, a sufferer, or an aggressor. For a moment or two, you were busy enough to forget the severity of the situation.

In a recent counseling session I confronted a bright Christian woman, Gina, who is married to Douglas, a chronic marijuana addict. For more than 20 years, she has suffered with his extreme moods and irresponsible behaviors. Gina learned long ago that one way to deal with them was simply not to talk about them, to ignore the "elephant in the room" that no one wants to acknowledge. To cope, she has busied herself in church-related activities that fulfill her and help her forget the craziness at home. Although her activities are vibrant and dynamic, she uses them to "forget," and that isn't healthy. I encouraged Gina to remember the issues at home that need attention. Ignoring the craziness won't make it go away. In fact, the problem will continue to grow and become even more debilitating.

Cleaning up messes. Crazy-makers create problems. They wreak havoc. Their paths are strewn with trouble in one form or another. You know it and perhaps have fallen into the habit of cleaning up their messes. You have learned not only to pick up the pieces, but also to put them back together again. A casual observer wouldn't know the problem existed in the first place. But every time you come to the rescue, you enable the crazy-maker to continue the same behavior pattern.

Not discussing problems. Most partners of crazy-makers practice the fine art of tiptoeing. You have learned not to talk directly about things. Oh, you may have tried. But crazy-makers don't want to be held accountable. Their smokescreens are very effective, so you find yourself not telling it like it is. You don't want to admit that you're not telling the truth to them, even though that is precisely what they need.

Not holding crazy-makers accountable. Perhaps you have been able to talk to crazy-makers. Perhaps you have had frank discussions—but progress stops there. You fail to really hold them accountable. Accountability is a four-letter word to crazy-makers. You threaten, warn, and rage, but you never set the bottom line, so the craziness continues. Tough love may require sharp edges—edges that indicate you will not tolerate certain behaviors. Edges that insist on couples counseling or treatment. Edges that say you will walk away when someone is demeaning you.

Not getting help. Holding the crazy-maker accountable is tough enough. To make matters worse, you try to go it alone. This is a sure-fire recipe for failure. You need the perspective of trusted counselors and confidants. Issues stay muddled when they remain in our heads. As a friend of mine reminded me recently, "The mind is a dangerous place. Don't go in there alone."

Ending Enabling

This book wouldn't be helpful if we simply spent our time lamenting the difficulties of interacting with crazy-makers. We have all had that experience time and again. We also wouldn't accomplish anything if we kept pointing the finger of responsibility outside ourselves—toward crazy-makers. Oh sure, they're difficult. Okay, they're impossible. But if we stop the finger-pointing, we're left feeling powerless and victimized. We must take back the ground we've given away. We must learn new skills to help us break free. But exactly how do we stop enabling their behavior?

Stop making excuses for them. That means absolutely no more excuses for their irresponsibility. No more excuses for their laziness around the house. Instead of telling yourself that he can't help being a control freak because his father was the same way, demand accountability.

Tell yourself the truth. You've been insisting that he or she tell the truth. That's fine, but you're better off starting with yourself. So, what is the truth of the matter? Is your mate a card-carrying aggressor who needs anger management or an egotist who needs you to stand firm in the face of his dominance? If you start with the truth, other healthy actions will naturally follow.

Don't pick up the pieces. Don't pay their overdue bills. Don't cover up for their workaholism. Let him explain to the kids where he was during their last soccer match. Look critically at all the ways you make the home run smoother by doing things that simply enable negative behavior. Consider where you can let things go, especially things that he or she will feel.

Don't make threats you won't carry out. Making idle threats causes you to lose crazy-makers' respect. Establish logical consequences and then follow through with them. No lectures. No lingering warnings. Just simple and clear consequences that you follow through with.

If she fails to pay the PUD bill for two months in a row, insist on talking together to the PUD accounts manager. If he blows up again, insist he seek anger management counseling. If he tries to control your activities, make clear that you will not be controlled and will continue to be sensitive to his desires without catering to his insecurities.

The crazy-maker will take you much more seriously if you establish rules that include accountability and consequences. Remember, a boundary has sharp edges—if you say you will no longer listen to someone yelling at you, walk away. If you say you will not tolerate someone threatening you, leave until you see changes. If you say you won't put up with your mother talking to you about your siblings, hang up the phone.

Refuse to lie or keep secrets. Commit to tell the truth—to yourself and to others. No more sugarcoating the problem. If his controlling behavior is making you crazy, tell someone. Don't call it anything other than what it is. Name it and be willing to come out of hiding and address it. Shame only exists in secret.

End your codependence. In my book *When Pleasing Others Is Hurting You,* I discuss the issue of codependence and the destructive impact it has on your personality and your relationships. John Bradshaw, in his book *Homecoming,* says, "To be codependent is to be out of touch with one's feelings, needs, and desires."[1] This happens insidiously when we live in relation to someone else's needs, opinions, and feelings. Stop living in fear of crazy-makers' feelings and actions. Live internally, according to what is true and right for you and according to what God is impressing upon you.

Drs. Hemfelt, Minirth, and Meier, in their book *Love Is a Choice,* identify ten traits of a codependent:

- The codependent is driven by one or more compulsions.
- The codependent is bound and often tormented by the way things were in the dysfunctional family of origin.
- The codependent's self-esteem (and frequently, maturity) is very low.
- A codependent is certain his or her happiness hinges on others.
- A codependent feels inordinately responsible for others.
- A codependent's relationship with a spouse or significant other is marred by a damaging, unstable lack of balance between dependence and independence.
- The codependent is a master of denial and repression.
- The codependent worries about things he or she can't change but may try to change anyway.
- A codependent's life is punctuated by extremes.
- A codependent is constantly looking for something that is missing or lacking in life.[2]

This list may seem foreboding at first glance. The important thing is to begin by identifying the problem and creating a strategy for dealing with it. Codependence does not get better with time. Changing these patterns requires a great deal of commitment.

Get support for yourself. No more going it alone. Come out of hiding and ask for help. Find a codependency support group and begin participating. Seek individual counseling if he or she refuses to join you. When we share our concerns in a support group, the issue loses some of its power over us.

The Freedom of Awakening

I have emphasized the importance of alertness when dealing with crazy-makers. Their number one tactic in hooking you is to catch you unawares. If you are mesmerized by their aggressive or manipulative behavior, you are vulnerable. This must change. Breaking free from the crazy-maker requires awakening, becoming observant, and noticing how you become mesmerized, paralyzed, and hooked.

I recall a critical moment in my young adulthood. I was 19 and attending Bible school—the same school where I labored for months to find myself and my purpose in life. In a particularly poignant moment, sitting with friends discussing a moving chapel service, I had an epiphany. I suddenly felt, emotionally, the importance of what Christ had done for me. My eyes were opened in a profound and new way. As a child, I'd heard all the stories of how Christ had died for my sins. But now, as an adult, His life, death, and resurrection took on new meaning. He lived and died for me! I experienced an awakening that has had a lasting impact on my life and changed the way I view the world. My understanding went from head knowledge to heart knowledge—the 24-inch drop from my head to my heart!

I am reminded of the story of *Sleeping Beauty.* In this fairy tale, Princess Aurora sleeps under layers of dependency—dependency on her father, on the three good fairies, and then on the prince. King Stefan, her father, forgets to invite the evil Maleficent to Aurora's christening. Maleficent shows up anyway and lays a curse on the baby girl—she will be pricked by a needle and die. The fairy Merryweather is able to alter the curse of death to the curse of sleep. Aurora, along with everyone else in the castle, goes to sleep. Their lives depend on the kiss from the prince. Of course, the prince finds Aurora and kisses her, and the kingdom awakens. In a moment the princess grows up, and the couple lives happily ever after.

We must go through a similar awakening. We must become independent enough to trust ourselves. This does not mean we give up trusting others—far from it. But we do not look to others for our identity.

Michael Gurian talks about this in his book *Love's Journey:*

> If we don't separate from caregivers and go through the long process of finding out who we are, we make mates, children, religion, nature, and work into dependency objects. We remain in a power struggle with them for the rest of our lives…When we awaken, we see much of this individuality already in place within us, noticing and honoring it as we never have before; we also see what false selves we've had to create—we move out of them as much as possible, as if working our way out of a shell; and we seek to develop new ways of being individuals. Unless we awaken, these won't take place.[3]

Christians can choose another type of awakening—being born again. During a conversation with the Pharisee Nicodemus, Jesus said, "I tell you the truth, no one can see the kingdom of God unless he is born again" (John 3:3).

This was a conundrum to Nicodemus, as it is for many today. Jesus went on to say, "No one can enter the kingdom of God unless he is born of water and the Spirit" (John 3:5). We each have an opportunity for a profound spiritual awakening that will give us new eyes with which to see our situation.

The Freedom of Detachment and Individuality

When we believe our mates are responsible for our happiness, or that we can only find happiness if something or someone outside of us changes, we live a most precarious life. If we cannot be happy unless our crazy-making mates change their behaviors, and if we have chosen to remain in relationship with them, we can expect our lives to be miserable.

Such was the case many months ago for Jacqueline, a bright, young girl preparing to attend graduate school. Jacqueline came to see me about "relationship issues." At 24, she was goal-directed and looking ahead to a wonderful future. Her challenge was that her boyfriend, Jess, was a control freak. The difficulty, however, was not so much that he was controlling. The underlying problem was her reaction and response to his control.

Specifically, Jess wanted Jacqueline to give up her career plans, which would take her from our small town to Seattle. She would not be able to reach her career goals and stay in the local community. But Jess was threatened by her plans to leave the area, even though she reassured him she wanted to continue their relationship. That assurance did not satisfy him. He wanted her to settle for lesser goals and center her life around his budding electrical business.

"He's so insecure," Jacqueline lamented. "I hate the fact that he is so dependent on me. Grad school is only going to last two years. I can come home to visit every weekend. But that's not good enough for him. In fact, he's threatening to break up with me if I won't change my plans. I doubt he'd really do it, but that's how insecure and controlling he is. I don't know what to do."

"I think it comes down to how important your dreams are to you," I said. "It seems pretty clear that graduate school is a high priority. Now you need to negotiate something that works for both you and Jess."

"That's just it," she said. "He won't negotiate, and he won't consider any other possibilities."

"How do you feel about his refusal to bend on this issue?" I asked.

"I hate it, of course. I've never been with someone so controlling. It drives me nuts, but I don't know what to do."

"What do you mean when you say that you don't know what to do?"

"If I pursue my dreams, I'll lose him, and I don't want to do that.

If I stay here in town, I'll lose the goals I've had since I was a child. I want a career in broadcasting. I've known that since the first time I watched *Good Morning America* when I was a kid."

"As I see it, you're in danger of becoming too dependent on Jess by enabling him to be controlling. If your dream is as important as you say it is, I'd think he would be more flexible. You appear to be trying to reassure him, but maybe it's time to test the relationship a bit. My recommendation is that you detach from him and see what happens."

Jacqueline agreed she had to detach from Jess and establish her individuality. This did not mean that she no longer cared for him. However, she was in danger of being smothered by his controlling personality. If she didn't establish the importance of her needs now, she would risk being engulfed and manipulated by him to an even greater degree in the future. If that were to happen, it could eventually mean the end of their relationship. So for her own sanity and the possible longevity of their relationship, she had to detach from his worries and insecurities and do what seemed right to her.

As it turns out, Jess threatened to end their relationship when Jacqueline told him she would not back down. She held firm, and today they enjoy a much healthier relationship. Jess has accepted her individuality and, in fact, has grown to foster her dreams. They are still dating and have plans to be married in the fall, when Jacqueline graduates from graduate school. Both have found ways to alter their individual plans to build a relationship together.

Boundaries by Design

So many of the issues we've been exploring, which require that we deal effectively with crazy-makers, demand that we establish internal boundaries. Some time ago, Drs. Henry Cloud and John Townsend reminded us of some very important scriptural principles that have the power to free us from the destructive behavior of crazy-makers.

Cloud and Townsend's work is chronicled in the book *Boundaries,* in which they illustrate the importance of setting limits. They show us that God designed a world where we all are intended to live within prescribed boundaries. In the act of creation, God set the land apart from the seas, separated the mountains from the valleys, and made the animal kingdom separate from humankind. Boundaries are ordained and ordered by God.

God's instructions to mankind were clear: "Be fruitful and increase in number; fill the earth and subdue it. Rule over the fish of the sea and the birds of the air and over every living creature that moves on the ground" (Genesis 1:28). Cloud and Townsend make this note:

> Made in the image of God, we were created to take responsibility for certain tasks. Part of taking responsibility, or ownership, is knowing what is our job, and what isn't. Workers who continually take on duties that aren't theirs will eventually burn out. It takes wisdom to know what we should be doing and what we shouldn't. We can't do everything.[4]

Knowing what is our business and what is not is a huge issue, particularly when dealing with the crazy-makers in our lives. Jacqueline was confused about boundaries in her relationship with Jess. She wanted to make him happy, but his version of happiness required that she give up her individuality. If she had not established boundaries in the early stages of their relationship, she would have lost respect for Jess and for herself. She would never have been truly happy, and their relationship would have suffered as a result.

Cloud and Townsend suggest that answering the following questions can be a great first step for people who are attempting to establish healthy boundaries. Consider your response to them:

- Can I set limits and still be a loving person?
- What are legitimate boundaries?
- What if someone is upset or hurt by my boundaries?
- How do I answer someone who wants my time, love, energy, or money?
- How do boundaries relate to submission?
- Aren't boundaries selfish?[5]

Perhaps you have wrestled with these same questions. I know I have and still do to this day. Let's see if we can answer them.

First, you can set limits and still be loving. In fact, setting limits is a loving act. Imagine what would happen if you did not set limits. What if you literally said yes to every request that came along?

Not long ago a young man befriended me at a book signing. He was disabled and desperately wanted a friend. He felt a special connection to me and wanted us to spend time together. As I considered his request to have coffee and chat, I had to weigh it against my other obligations. I reluctantly decided that to make time for this young man would cheat others in my life. Our choices in one direction limit our choices in another. As much as I'd like to do it all—to be a friend to everyone, to answer each and every e-mail and letter in detail—I cannot. My time and energy are limited, and I have a responsibility to make healthy choices in favor of those God has called to be in my life.

We would do well to learn from the parable of the orchardist in the Scripture. Remember Jesus' teaching: "He cuts off every branch in me that bears no fruit, while every branch that does bear fruit he prunes" (John 15:2). This verse tells me that there is a time to say no to good things so that what remains can be even more fruitful.

Second, what are legitimate boundaries? Legitimate boundaries are those we have a responsibility to protect. We have the responsibility to manage and care for our emotions, our behaviors, our attitudes and beliefs, as well as our friendships and activities. As we often hear in church, we are to use wise stewardship of our time, talents, and treasures.

Third, others will sometimes be upset by our boundaries. Boundaries have edges. I recall several years ago asking a friend if I could borrow his truck for the day. He firmly said, "No, I will be needing my truck." Not to be deterred, I asked him if I could borrow the truck for a few hours. Again, he said, "No, I will be needing my truck." But I wouldn't take no for an answer. I told him I would have it back to him promptly if he would just loan it to me for a short time. My friend said curtly, "David, what part of 'no' don't you understand?"

I've remembered the event as much for my stubbornness as for his firmness. My hurt feelings were my responsibility. He did nothing to feel bad about. Boundaries have edges, and once in a while they sting—especially when people put you on the spot.

Fourth, you must be a good steward of your time, love, energy, and money. You have only so much of each to go around, and you alone are responsible for how you disperse them. You do not have unlimited time, for example, and if you choose to give it to a friend, you will not have it to give to someone else. The same is true of your money. You could give it away, but that would be poor stewardship. Crazy-makers will find a way to demand your resources, but their request rarely lead to worthwhile investments of your resources. Spending our time and talents wisely yields a good return. You must be mindful of how you choose to use them.

Fifth, both husbands and wives—and everyone else, for that matter—should practice submission. Submission is not something for people to use as a weapon against their spouses. Rather, it is something given freely to model and more fully experience Christ's love. The Scriptures don't tell us that one partner is intended to have control over another. In fact, the model is to "submit to one another out of reverence for Christ" (Ephesians 5:21).

Sixth, establishing boundaries is not a selfish act. Consider what Cloud and Townsend have to say on this matter:

> Appropriate boundaries actually increase our ability to care about others. People with highly developed limits are the most caring people on earth...A helpful way to understand setting limits is that our lives are a gift from God. Just as a store manager takes good care of a shop for the owner, we are to do the same with our souls. If a lack of boundaries causes us to mismanage the store, the owner has a right to be upset with us.[6]

If we allow them to do so, crazy-makers will hook us into frittering away our time, love, energy, and money. Therefore, we practice good stewardship when we set limits on how we allow crazy-makers to treat us.

The Freedom of Decision

To be a successful steward of your boundaries, you will need to make some important decisions. You must acknowledge that your boundaries are very personal, and you have a responsibility to guard and protect them. This is not selfish behavior; it is simply your responsibility.

Most humans are rational beings, and we have the ability and the power to make choices. Along with that ability, of course, comes responsibility. We will reap what we sow.

Breaking free from crazy-makers, whether you choose to leave them or take control of your interactions with them, will require making some difficult decisions. It will involve changing your own behaviors. As you become mindful of these new behaviors, you can feel empowered by them.

John Bradshaw, an author who has significantly influenced me, wrote in his book *Homecoming* that it is never too late to have a happy childhood. By that, he means that through new, healthier decisions, we can care for the child within us, raising him or her in healthier ways. Bradshaw suggests that we need to consider new avenues for caring for our boundaries. Doing so will make us healthier.

Consider some of the decisions you can make today to create healthier boundaries in your life:

- Decide that you are responsible to set healthy boundaries regarding your time, talents, resources, body, and spiritual well-being.
- Decide to practice maintaining those healthy boundaries, protecting them as you would your own home.
- Ask for wisdom from God to help you in this endeavor.
- Associate with people who will show care, concern, and respect for those boundaries.
- Show care, concern, and respect for others' boundaries and their efforts to live healthier lives.

Choosing Our Friends

Henri Nouwen, noted theologian and author, has much to say

about decision making, boundaries, and the healthy spiritual life. He suggests in his book *Here and Now* that our well-being is a matter of spiritual and emotional importance and must be guarded fiercely.

> The spiritual life is one of constant choices. One of the most important choices is the choice of people with whom we develop close intimate relationships. We have only a limited amount of time in our lives. With whom do we spend it and how? That's probably one of the most decisive questions of our lives…To whom do we go to for advice? With whom do we spend our free evenings? Sometimes we speak or act as if we have little choice in the matters. Sometimes we act as though we will be lucky if there is anyone who wants to be our friend. But that is a passive and fatalistic attitude.[7]

We will have many opportunities for friendships. Nouwen encourages us to choose wisely. Have we prayed about these friendships? What kinds of friends do we need at this time in our life?

God knows and cares about the people who need to be in our life for this season for this reason. But the choice is ours, and we must choose wisely.

Boundary Checklist

You may still be wondering whether you have established healthy boundaries. Remember, setting limits on the impact of crazy-makers in your life is critical. Here are a few questions, taken from Dr. Charles Whitfield's book *Boundaries and Relationships,* that you can use to evaluate your progress:

- Am I able to say no to requests?
- Am I able to understand that my happiness does not depend on other people?
- Do I find myself involved with people who end up hurting me?
- Can I choose friends whom I trust to care for me?
- Do I consider my opinion to be as important as others'?

- Do people take or use my things without my permission?
- Can I ask others for what I want and need?
- Do I go along with other people rather than voicing my desires?
- Do I feel proud of being an individual with unique qualities?
- Have I found a balance between helping others and meeting my own needs?
- Am I able to determine what I think and believe?
- Am I able to make effective decisions?
- Am I able to get out of relationships that continue to hurt me?
- Am I able to stay out of other's problems?
- Am I able to sort out my own feelings and thoughts as separate from others?
- Do I understand that I am not responsible for other people's feelings?[8]

Developing healthy boundaries may be a new venture for you, so it is likely to be a challenge. This checklist may have helped you become aware of areas in your life that need more work.

Don't lose heart. You can learn to honor and protect your boundaries. These skills will have a powerful impact on your ability to deal with the crazy-makers in your life.

Summary

Setting boundaries may be the most important set of skills for dealing with the crazy-maker. Boundaries define who you are and who you aren't. They deliver a clear statement to crazy-makers, letting them know that they are free to act however they choose but that you will make healthy choices in response to their actions.

With practice, setting boundaries will give you a level of freedom you may have never known. You will be able to take the power out of the hands of the crazy-maker and place it squarely back where it belongs—with you.

11

The Freedom
of Normalcy

*Often people attempt to live their lives backwards: they
try to have more things, or more money, in order to do
more of what they want so that they will be happier.
They way it actually works is the reverse. You must first
be who you really are, then, do what you need to do, in
order to have what you want.*

MARGARET YOUNG

"How would you know?" the patient yelled at me. "You're a normie!"

"A what?" I asked.

"A normie," he repeated. "You've never been an addict or an alcoholic. You don't know what it's like to live in a crazy world every day of your life."

I was the psychologist on a drug and alcohol inpatient unit, trying to help men and women get clean and sober. And this man was absolutely right. I'm a normie. I have not lived a single day of my life searching for drugs or craving alcohol, nor have I lived amid the chaos associated with dysfunctional families.

Although the alcoholic man sounded angry with me, I knew

that beneath his apparent irritation, other feelings were stirring the mix. He undoubtedly yearned for normalcy. He longed for the day when drugs and alcohol did not dominate his thoughts. No doubt he wanted a life of predictability, and he might just have it, depending on his success in treatment.

During my three years on the unit, I watched people come and go. Some entered the unit swearing that they had hit the bottom and were ready for change, only to leave AMA—against medical advice—because the recovery process was too difficult and the temptations too strong.

My time with these suffering folks left me with unforgettable stories. I heard tales of pain and anguish. Stories of broken relationships, lost jobs, empty bank accounts, and craziness—the kind of craziness we've been talking about in this book.

I worked hard to help these people face the challenges of their addiction and recovery. I helped them confront their "stinkin' thinking," the kind of illogical thinking we talked about in previous chapters. They would need renewed minds if recovery were to have a fighting chance.

As I looked around our meeting room week after week, month after month, I made a powerful observation: Many of these people had never known normalcy in their lives. They simply did not know what being normal was like, and subsequently they had no idea how to find the path that would take them there.

I have never spent my time trying to buy drugs or wondering where I had stashed the last bottle of wine, but I have lived in my own crazy world of work addiction. I have obsessed about pleasing a referral source, attended numerous business network meetings, and handed out thousands of business cards, always focused on work, success, and personal image. Because I have traveled through the land of obsessions and compulsions, I discovered that my world wasn't so distant from the one the addicts I was counseling inhabited.

One major difference, however, is that I haven't known their world of chaos. I haven't been enmeshed in a family filled with addicts, borderlines, and aggressors. I haven't lived with egotists or been forced to endure sufferers. I have also not spent much time with control freaks. I have had the good grace of being protected by my family of origin from much of the crazy-making discussed in this book.

I guess the patient was right—even with all my quirks, concerns, frustrations, and discouragements, I am a normie. In this chapter we will explore normalcy—what it is and what it isn't. Most important, we will learn what it takes to be normal and how that will help us with crazy-makers.

Never Knowing Normalcy

As I write this book, I try to understand what living with crazy-makers is like. As I described in an earlier chapter, the business network dinner at my home included an egotist, aggressor, sufferer, borderline, and control freak. We were together in the same room for an entire evening. But I don't live with them every day.

What is living with a control freak like? Living every day with someone who insists on telling you what to do and how to do it? What is it like to be married to an aggressor—someone who uses anger and hostility to manipulate you? And what about life with the borderline, where a wild ride at Disney World seems like a walk in the park by comparison? You may be living in one of these situations. Your passion for healing drives me to write, to study, to try to experience—if even for a moment—what you are experiencing. I want my words to be relevant.

What if these crazy-makers have never known anything but what they see and experience at this moment? "A fish is the last one to see the water." I am quite certain it is the same with the crazy-makers—they are the last ones to truly see how crazy they make their world.

I have heard that the best way to discover counterfeit money is to study bona fide currency. If you know what the real thing looks like, detecting counterfeit currency is relatively easy. Together we can explore what being normal means and how we can seek normalcy in our lives. We can explore what life would be like never having known normalcy and the impact craziness has on one's development. We will discuss what happens to people who are around crazy-makers much of their life. Then we will discover how to find normalcy.

Living in Abnormalcy

Crazy-makers live in abnormalcy. They live in a backward world, where up may very well mean down, where right means left, and sadly, bad may mean good. Everything is distorted. You know this because you probably have crazy-makers in your life. But the greatest tragedy is that this seems customary to them. They often don't know any difference, and they almost certainly don't know the profound impact they have on you.

People living in abnormalcy have learned a wide set of dys-functional behaviors. According to Dr. Albert Bernstein, they "are not intrinsically evil, but their immaturity allows them to operate without thinking about whether their actions are good or bad." They see others as potential sources for whatever they happen to need at the moment, not as separate human beings with needs and feelings of their own. Bernstein says that understanding their immaturity is your ultimate goal because "many of their outrageous actions would make perfect sense if they were done by a two-year-old."[1]

Let's briefly review what Bernstein is talking about and what we have focused on throughout this book.

Aggressors have developed abnormal, aggressive tendencies. As a result, they are inclined to intimidate others with their rage reactions. They are truly like two-year-olds, acting belligerent, demanding, and outrageously immature. Their drug of choice is rage because it temporarily makes them strong. Their anger paralyzes others, giving aggressors power and control. Without it, they feel ineffective.

Anne Lamott tells of her encounter with an aggressor in her book *Traveling Mercies*. She was walking the beach with her son Sam and the family dog when a man with a golden retriever approached them. Everything was fine until his dog didn't obey him.

> And the man picked up a thick stick from the ground,
> and smashed it into his dog's rib cage. The dog flinched
> big time but did not even yelp. Sam did; Sam yelped from

fifteen feet away. It was absolutely stunning. All I could do was whisper, "No." Sadie [her dog] looked at the dog and then tore over to them. The retriever turned to watch her go, and the man hit her again in the ribs.

Anger and aggression are paralyzing. For a moment, life becomes surreal. We are not sure what to do, what to think, how to react. We are not prepared when grownups act like belligerent brats. We have half a mind to scream at them, turn them over our knees for a good spanking, or run away from them. Lamott shares her reaction.

> I didn't know if the man was evil or just violent. Lots of people are scary and dangerous because they are sick or stupid or powerful. Drugs and alcohol make people stupid and violent, but I don't think that necessarily makes them evil. Evil is when you choose to do such harm. So I don't know. We can't read other people's hearts. We just know what's in our own, what wrongs we're capable of, and that knowledge is terrible enough.[2]

Lamott's response is gracious, a sure sign of maturity. She is insightful, telling us later in the book how she too acts aggressively with her son at times. But, she adds, she feels sorry and makes amends for her actions. She is vulnerable enough to reveal to us her aggressive tendencies and perceptive enough to recognize them for what they are.

Anger is an effective tool for aggressors. In the long run, however, their behavior destroys them. Only when the bottom falls out of their lives do they see the full impact of their behavior. Until then, they'll keep pushing and snorting, attacking and demeaning others for the thrill of it—and for the power and control. This is abnormal behavior for anyone older than two.

Egotists are equally childlike and self-centered. In fact, if you're not hooked into their behavior, it can appear quite humorous. With their chests puffed out, they act like they own the world. Everything they say is the truth, and they expect you to bow down and honor them. Their egos fill the room. If they hook you, however, it is serious business. They are firmly convinced that they are better than anyone else. They love competition, but they are poor losers. They have little interest in what others are thinking and feeling because those thoughts and feelings may not place them at center stage. This behavior is antisocial, abnormal, and crazy-making.

The borderline is especially immature and volatile, like a tempestuous two-year-old who has been spoiled far too long. You must walk on eggshells if you want to avoid a blast of rage from the borderline. You find yourself guarding your thoughts because borderlines are likely to overreact to something you say. They twist your words to conform to the meaning they choose. You are on high alert, not knowing if your words or actions will bring on an emotional storm that transforms you from best friend to worst enemy.

In a therapy group I conducted recently, I watched a black-and-white scenario unfold in a matter of seconds. I was listening to Rachel, a vibrant redhead dressed in blue jeans and sweatshirt, talk about being laid off from her job. She was annoyed at the employer for letting her go without an explanation, and she was frightened about her finances.

"Did you talk to your boss about his decision and ask if you could do anything to save your job?" I asked.

"Do you think I'm stupid?" she snarled. "Of course I talked to him. But he didn't want to talk to me. I didn't do anything wrong."

This blast from the borderline was more than enough to make me consider whether I would tolerate any more of this behavior. It also told me that Rachel had probably lost her job for some very specific and legitimate reasons!

In a matter of seconds I went from being a good psychologist to a bad one; from feeling safe and respected to feeling attacked and distrusting. This is how people feel who are subject to the abnormal and crazy-making world of the borderline.

Sufferers are also quite childlike and abnormal. They have failed to take a critical step—becoming independent. They spend much of their time and energy getting others to take care of them, feel sorry for them, and grant them more time, money, and attention.

Their problems are bigger and far more dramatic than yours. Although they certainly struggle with self-esteem, in a twisted way they are also grandiose in letting you know that your problems in no way rival theirs.

When interacting with a sufferer, you will often feel drained. Some people are energy givers, and others are energy takers. Sufferers most certainly take, and that is not acceptable behavior for mature adults.

Control freaks are not necessarily childish, although they are immature and abnormal. Like egotists, control freaks must have their way. And their way is the only way. Their bizarre behavior demonstrates their lack of balance and reciprocity. They do not live as most of us do, in a world with an equilibrium between give and take. They have forgotten the "give" part and fully emphasize the "take." Because they feel extraordinarily entitled, they expect things to be done to their satisfaction, but they fail to consider your satisfaction. Subsequently, you end up feeling small when around them. Because their ideas are of utmost importance, your ideas don't matter. Although they may occasionally make you believe they are listening, you never really feel that they are hearing or understanding you. Their view of the world, like their manner of dealing with people, is not healthy.

Crazy-Maker Osmosis

Living in a world of crazy-makers can make you feel and perhaps even act crazy yourself. I call this "crazy-making osmosis."

When Rachel lambasted me in the therapy group, my first reaction was paralysis. My second reaction was anger. I try to be self-conscious and mature enough to act in a dignified and professional manner, but that doesn't always happen.

When Rachel accused me of being stupid, I should have said, "I'm sorry, Rachel. I can tell that losing your job is very upsetting for you." But I didn't. Instead, I shot back, "Geez, Rachel. You don't have to attack me. I'm just asking a question. Do you have something you're not telling us?"

My comments were not helpful, mature, or therapeutic. I had been hooked and found myself experiencing crazy-making osmosis—her childish behavior had sucked me into immature behavior.

We commonly act like the people we are around. Thus, if we are with an aggressor, we may find ourselves acting just as aggressively as he acts. If we are with someone who is dependent and whiny, such as a sufferer, we may find ourselves acting dependent as well. And if we spend time with the volatility of the borderline, we may overreact at times.

Crazy-making osmosis also works in an opposite manner. Instead of reacting forcefully with the aggressor, you may have difficulty expressing any kind of anger. Anger may frighten you into suppressing any dissatisfaction. Instead of being volatile like the borderline, you may feel you have to be steady and stable, never losing your cool. If you have grown up with a dependent parent or been with a dependent partner, you may feel as if you have to be independent and strong. In other words, you overcompensate for their immaturity—and thus act abnormally.

Listen to this excerpt of two women talking about their mothers, taken from Nora Roberts' book *Blue Dahlia*. The scene starts with Stella coming into Roz's office for a business meeting.

> Roz leaned back in her chair, crossed her sock-covered feet at the ankles. "Is there a problem?"
>
> "So much for the illusion that I conceal my emotions under a composed façade. No, no problem. I did the duty call home to my mother a little while ago. I'm still recovering...My mama spent most of her time—at least the time we were on earth together—sighing wistfully over her health. Not that she meant to complain, so she said. I very nearly put that on her tombstone. 'Not That I Meant to Complain.'"
>
> "I could put 'I Don't Ask for Much' on my mother's."
>
> "There you go. Mine made such an impression on me that I went...in the opposite direction. I could probably cut off a limb, and you wouldn't hear a whimper out of me."[3]

Have you been drawn into behaviors and thinking patterns typical of our group of crazy-makers? Have you moved dramatically in the opposite direction as a means of overcompensation?

- Do you find yourself acting aggressively with aggressors?
- Do you find yourself avoiding an expression of any kind of anger?
- Do you have a hard time saying no to them?
- Do you react temperamentally with borderlines?
- Do you overreact to situations?
- Do you feel you have to be strong and stable because of others' temperamental natures?
- Do you have difficulty managing your emotions?
- Do you shrink back when with egotists?
- Do you have a hard time championing your own accomplishments?
- Do you find yourself being strong when with sufferers?
- Do you try to buoy their sagging emotions?
- Do you defend or overly explain yourself with control freaks?
- Do you give up your opinion with egotists and control freaks?

If you said yes to any of the questions above, you may not simply have been hooked by the crazy-maker—you may actually be changing your personality. You not only feel hooked but may be taking on dysfunctional personality traits. If so, you'll need to be clear about those traits and consciously endeavor to make changes toward normalcy.

Seeking Normalcy

You now have a good idea of what abnormalcy is and can readily identify the traits of various crazy-makers. Let's shift our attention to normalcy, examining both what it looks like and how to attain it.

Patricia Evans, in her book *Controlling People,* gives us a compass by which we can measure our emotional well-being. Drawing from the personality theory of Carl Jung, Evans notes that everyone is born with four functions—feeling, sensate, intuitive, and thinking. These functions are the basis of the Myers-Briggs Personality Indicator, a popular test among educators, career counselors, and psychologists. Consider how these functions operate together.

When Gail and Ben came in for their initial counseling session with me, they both took a moment to look around the room. Gail commented on my water fountain and Ben remarked about the view of the Cowlitz River. (Both were using the sensate function.)

As we began our session, I asked them to share why they had sought out counseling. They looked at one another, examining each other's expression and gauging each other's mood (using the feeling function). Ben commented that he and Gail were doing better in their relationship since the time they called for their appointment (using the thinking function) but also noted that he feared they could slip back into the type of troubling behavior that had prompted the call in the first place (using the intuitive function).

Gail started the session. She was quite animated as she shared that she and Ben had been married for nearly ten years and had two young children. Their angry outbursts sometimes threatened the health of their relationship. During these outbursts, they commonly engaged in power struggles over what she admitted were inconsequential issues.

"I don't even know why we fight about the things we do," she said. "It's stupid. Neither of us likes fighting, but we know that arguments are sometimes unavoidable. We need a tune-up to make sure we're fighting fair."

"How about you?" I said to Ben.

"I agree. We both grew up with parents who fought all the time. We hate arguing, yet we find ourselves doing it too often. I'm starting a new business, and I know that's creating some of the pressure. We're here to find out how we can handle it better."

Ben and Gail were wise in their decision to seek counseling to maintain the communication skills they had developed during their ten-year marriage. They had been in counseling before, they noted, and it had benefited them. They had a pattern of fighting that was destructive, and they wanted to ensure that their marriage didn't deteriorate. Obviously, they prized their relationship.

Both Ben and Gail utilized their four functions to make the decision to give their marriage a "tune-up." They used their sensate function to determine something was wrong. They could sense tension mounting, and they realized they needed to find a way to de-escalate.

Ben and Gail also had a refined feeling function, which let them know they were angry and hurt and didn't want to stay that way. They obviously cared for one another and wanted harmony back in their home.

Patricia Evans says, "The emotions we experience through our feeling function help us to know who and what we are, what is good for us and what is not. Our ability to empathize with others depends on our feeling function along with our other functions."[4]

Ben and Gail used their intuitive function to attend to the trouble at hand. Their feelings, intuition, and sensations informed them that they had some relational work to do. Although they weren't sure exactly what they needed to do, they knew they were in trouble. The time had come to reach out for help, which prompted a call to my office.

They also accessed a secondary source of information, apart from direct experience—the thinking function. Prior to coming to my office, they had discussed their situation. Using refined, abstract reasoning abilities, they were able to make sense out of what was happening. Ben knew he was under unusual pressure from starting his new construction business. They discussed the pressures of having two preschool-age children and the financial pressures that were weighing the family down.

As I listened to Ben and Gail share their story, I couldn't help thinking that they were already ahead of the game. Together they had already thought about their circumstances, reasoned out their problems, and realized that they needed extra assistance. By using their thinking function, they were able to assimilate information from their other three functions and perform active problem solving.

You might be thinking that Ben and Gail are unique, and you are right. Who volunteers for counseling before a crisis develops? Who sits down, reasons out their problems, and puts together even a partial plan before reaching the counseling office?

Ben and Gail were indeed unusual because they were allies united in their quest for a healthier relationship. They could be called normies because of the skills they already possessed.

The Danger of Disconnection

When associating with crazy-makers, you are in danger of disconnecting from one or all of the four normal functions you need to be healthy and free. And if you disconnect, you may take on abnormal traits.

Consider an experience that is played out thousands of times in crazy-makers' homes.

A seven-year-old comes home from school, discouraged because she wasn't invited to her friend's birthday party. Her mother says, "Oh, it doesn't really matter. She's just being selfish. You didn't want to be her friend anyway."

How is that child going to develop? Her mother's statement invalidated her perceptions, and her declaration that this rejection didn't matter was the exact opposite of the truth. The mother presented the experience to the girl backward. Can you imagine what the girl might have been thinking, and perhaps what would have liked to say, had she been older and more mature?

"Mother, you're wrong. It does really matter. Yes, my friend is being selfish, but I do want to be her friend."

Sadly, this child will probably learn to disconnect from her four primary functions. Her world will take on an increasingly distorted, abnormal shape. If her mother doesn't change, this little girl will learn to distrust or stifle what she sees, altering her sensate function; ignore what she thinks, denying her thinking function; limit her hunches or intuitive function; and repress her emotions or feeling function.

Consider what happens when this child's experience is repeated many times over while growing up and then again as an adult. What happens to this child as she grows into adulthood and perhaps marries an aggressor who continues the process of telling her what to think and do?

The young woman, now married, is harried and working hard to care for her young children as well as manage the duties of their home. Having learned to deny her inner world of feelings and thoughts, she lives in reaction to other's needs. Her husband, the aggressor, comes home tired and irritable.

"Why is the house such a mess?" he asks angrily.

"You're not being fair," she replies automatically. "I've been working all day, and I'm exhausted. The kids take more energy than you think."

"That's no excuse," he says. "I work all day too, and your job isn't nearly as hard as mine. I don't see why you can't handle your easy job and the house."

"Well, I'm exhausted," she says, "and I can't help it. There is a lot to do around here, and I could use a hand from you."

"You shouldn't be so tired," he scoffs. "You don't even know what hard work is."

Just as in her childhood, her thoughts, feelings, and perceptions are invalidated and distorted, but this time by an angry aggressor. She gradually learns she must disconnect herself from her sensate awareness that something is wrong. She must disconnect from her feeling awareness, or she will become discouraged and depressed. She must disconnect from her intuitive awareness or she will realize that she is in danger. She must disconnect from her thinking awareness; she must not reason too much, or she will be told she is not making sense. Someone else, in this case her husband, now has the power to take away her freedom. With this abuse occurring repeatedly, he has the power to redefine her inner reality.

The Four Freedoms

If gradual disconnection is the culprit, gradual reconnection is the answer. If crazy-makers cause disconnection, the answer is a courageous reconnection to the four functions or, as I like to call them, the four freedoms.

What would your life be like if instead of being invalidated by the crazy-maker in your life and perhaps even yourself, you were validated? What if you honored and freely affirmed your feelings, sensations, intuition, and thinking? I can tell you the answer. Your world would begin to make sense again. You would know what you know, feel what you feel, intuit what you intuit, and think what you think. With these skills and natural abilities, you could make healthy decisions. You would redefine and transform your inner world—and maybe your outer world as well.

John Bradshaw elaborates on the theme of honoring our innate, God-given freedoms. He outlines what he refers to as "nurturing rules" as a way of returning to normalcy. Through these ten rules, based heavily on the four freedoms, you will rediscover normalcy—or perhaps find it for the first time. With practice you will find these guidelines incredibly healing.

1. Feeling what you feel is okay. Feelings are not right or wrong, they just are. No one can tell you what you should feel. However, talking about feelings is good and necessary.

2. Wanting what you want and asking for it is okay. Getting your needs met is necessary.

3. Seeing and hearing what you see and hear is okay.

4. Having fun is okay and necessary.

5. Telling the truth at all times is essential. This will reduce life's pain. Lying distorts reality.

6. Knowing your limits and delaying gratification is sometimes important. This will also reduce life's pain.

7. Developing a balanced sense of responsibility is crucial. This means accepting the consequences for what you do and refusing to accept the consequences for what someone else does.

8. Making mistakes is okay. Mistakes are our teachers—they help us to learn.

9. We need to respect and value other people's feelings,

needs, and wants. Violation leads to guilt and other hurtful consequences.

10. Having problems and conflict is okay. However, we need to recognize and resolve them.[5]

How did you fare as you reviewed these traits of normalcy? Are your relationships largely positive and normal, or are they primarily dysfunctional? Imagine the benefits that would result if everyone practiced the four freedoms as well as these ten nurturing rules.

Going Sane

Sanity is like a breath of fresh air. We've spent too much time letting crazy-makers hook us, and now it's time to focus our energies on becoming normal.

I first discovered the term *crazy-makers* in Julia Cameron's book, *The Artist's Way*, where she offers this description:

> Crazy-makers are those personalities that create storm centers. They are often charismatic, frequently charming, highly inventive, and powerfully persuasive. And, for the creative person in your vicinity, they are highly destructive. You know the type: charismatic but out of control, long on problems and short on solutions. Crazy-makers are the kind of people who can take over your whole life.[6]

Cameron offers a number of insights about how to get some distance from those who would destroy your creative genius. She says, "Survival lies in sanity, and sanity lies in paying attention…The quality of life is in proportion, always, to the capacity for delight. The capacity for delight is the gift of paying attention."[7]

Gail and Ben paid attention. They noticed something had slipped in their marriage. They were not able to put their finger on the problem, but they realized that they needed to seek help. Their reward for paying attention was catching their problems before they escalated and created more damage. They renewed skills that minimized conflict and recovered their joy.

When we pay close attention to our lives, we notice what brings us joy and what causes us grief. This connection will pay rich dividends.

How are you doing at paying attention to your life? Where might you still be disconnected? In our list of freedoms and rules, which pose the greatest challenges for you today?

If you pay attention, with God's grace and help, you can recover, change, and grow.

A Spiritual Compass

A discussion of normalcy would be incomplete without the authority of the Word of God. What humankind calls normal or wise is incomplete—perhaps even askew—without the wisdom of God. "For the wisdom of this world is foolishness in God's sight" (1 Corinthians 3:19).

We must keep everything in perspective. The freedoms and rules we've discussed are right and true only insofar as they do not violate God's standards and truths.

Returning to normalcy after living in the shadow of a crazy-maker includes learning to trust yourself again. However, if you don't have a spiritual compass that you can trust, you may still be heading off course. To be safe, you will need to find your bearings in the Scriptures. As you immerse yourself in the Scriptures you will maintain a healthy focus—a true and right bearing for your life.

As the apostle Paul says, "Whatever is true, whatever is noble, whatever is right, whatever is pure, whatever is lovely, whatever is admirable—if anything is excellent or praiseworthy—think about such things" (Philippians 4:8).

In our final chapter, we will discuss how God is the basis and source of strength as we consider the costs, courage, and challenges of real change.

12

Total Freedom: Catch and Release

Those who deny freedom to others deserve it not for themselves.

ABRAHAM LINCOLN

For several years, my sons, my father, and I practiced an annual ritual. After my boys graduated from high school, I promised to take them, along with my dad, to the wilds of Alaska for a mega-fishing expedition. For those of us who live in the Pacific Northwest, Alaska is the epitome of untamed, unmanaged mystique—that last frontier that every kid is dying to visit.

My oldest son Joshua, my father, and I made the first excursion. It was a magnificent adventure that included several fly-in destinations, where we were sure to catch our limits of wild rainbow trout and perhaps even experience a not-too-close-for-comfort moment with a brown bear.

We flew into Anchorage in September 2000, and before heading out into the bush, we fished the Kenai River. What a time we had catching and releasing wild rainbow trout. For those unfamiliar with trout, these were big, bad boys—most in the seven- to nine-pound range. They put up an incredible fight, leaping out of the water and shaking their heads wildly in an effort to throw the hook. Though I knew it was "sustainable" to "catch and release," another part of me wanted to hook 'em and keep 'em.

The next day, we climbed aboard a rickety floatplane piloted by a bearded, longhaired guide and headed out over the tundra and countless lakes, many of which were rarely fished. Our guide swooped low over several river embankments to give us a view of brown bear feeding on spawning fish. I'm not sure what was more thrilling—the sight of brown bear standing sentry in the rivers or the quick dive of the floatplane. Both were incredibly exhilarating.

Half an hour later, we landed on a remote lake where we were promised a bounty of fish. We were not disappointed as the fish were large, plentiful, and full of fight. Again, however, we were told it was catch-and-release, which at the time, was a relatively new program put in place to save salmon and other fish. True sportsmen would gladly comply with such regulations, ensuring plenty of fish for years to come.

Two years later I made a similar trip with my youngest son Tyson and my father. We covered much the same territory with equally awe-inspiring results. We fished several rivers near Anchorage, primarily for sockeyes and pinks. We were allowed to catch and keep up to three salmon per day.

Sustainable

Catch-and-release is fine in the fishing world. However, being lured, hooked, snared, or caught in any manner by crazy-makers is not enjoyable, even if you find a way to secure your release. Every minute you spend on the crazy-makers' line is draining, even exhausting. And as you also know, it is completely preventable. With the right skills, you can avoid being hooked or find a way to quickly be released.

Environmental sustainability is an intriguing concept. Can we live in such a way that we leave the earth a better place for our children and grandchildren? And, pertaining to this book, what about emotional sustainability? Can we practice healthy boundaries with one another without ever getting hooked or manipulated by crazy-makers?

I believe in the concept of emotional sustainability—I want crazy-makers to come and go without leaving a trace on the rest of us. If that could happen—if we could have such a profound respect for each other that we would never want to hook each other, our world would drastically change. In the process, perhaps egotists, aggressors, sufferers, borderlines, and control freaks would lose their appetite for hooking us.

A Singular Purpose

Alaska's wild fish give the appearance of fighting fiercely for their freedom. Against enormous odds and obstacles, salmon migrate to the ocean, stay for several years, and then instinctively find their way back to the precise location where they were born. It is an incredible story that has the fingerprint of the Creator all over it. Salmon navigate hundreds of miles from the Pacific Ocean to their spawning grounds. Many are lost to predators and fishermen along the way. Some are caught and released. Some are hooked, caught, and bagged.

The salmon are driven by instinct. Their journey is written into their genetic code. Using their natural senses, they simply know which creek, river, or stream is home. They stop at nothing to retain their freedom until they return to the stream where they can spawn and then die. Theirs is a fight to the death.

I once took a tour bus into the mountains above Ketchikan, Alaska. We passed slowly by a crook in a river and watched bears hooking salmon, eating their heads, and tossing the carcasses back into the river. Fish after fish, the bears seldom required more than a swift, jerking motion to hook their meal. Some salmon escaped the danger. Many did not.

In some ways, the salmon's fight is similar to yours. They fight for freedom. They fight because it is in their DNA to do so. They fight to continue a life cycle designed by the Creator and perpetuated by acts of nature. Through trial and trouble, they pursue a singular purpose—to be free. It is in your DNA to be free as well, and I hope you will stop at nothing to gain that freedom.

The Desire to Change

At times, perhaps you feel as if you are swimming upstream through a feeding frenzy of hungry bears. When you see those paws the size of baseball mitts and claws like knives, you wonder if you stand a chance. But freedom is your destiny. It drives you forward. You know that being caught goes against what you know to be right, and you will settle for nothing less than survival and independence.

If crazy-makers affect your life, you no doubt have a desire to change so that you can be free. You are tired of being caught, even if you are eventually released. You wouldn't have read this far if you didn't want things to be drastically different. Now the question is, how badly do you want to change? A little bit of desire will not cut it. The transformation will require a monumental effort.

Gerald May, in his wonderful book *Addiction and Grace,* says that we often repress our desires.

> We try to keep our focus on other things—safer things…But something that has been repressed does not really go away; it remains with us, skirting the edge of our consciousness. Every now and then it reminds us of its presence, as if to say, "Remember me?" And, when we are ready to tackle the thing again, we can.[1]

Jesus talks a great deal about desire. In fact, He told two parables about desiring the kingdom of heaven.

> The kingdom of heaven is like treasure hidden in a field. When a man found it, he hid it again, and then in his joy went and sold all he had and bought that field. Again, the kingdom of heaven is like a merchant looking for fine pearls. When he found one of great value, he went away and sold everything he had and bought it (Matthew 13:44-46).

In both parables, the man is willing to give up everything in exchange for the desired treasure or pearl of great value. Think about it—giving everything in exchange for something you consider of utmost value. Is your freedom from crazy-making worth this much to you? Are you willing to give up the comfort and predictability you currently know in exchange for the discomfort that will surely accompany change?

My wife teases me about always being obsessed with the latest, greatest treasure. In recent months I've been preoccupied with vintage Vespas, VW Beetles, and house barges on the Seattle waterfront. I wrap my mind around these ideas, so much so that, at times, I can hardly think of anything else. I attribute it to raw desire.

That is the type of passion you need in order to free yourself from crazy-makers.

The Freedom to Change

We need to change in order to become free. We also need to be free to change. If our minds are attached to anything except Christ, we are not free. An obsession over anything hampers us to a certain degree in this quest. When watching a dog with a bone, we may wonder whether the dog has the bone or the bone has the dog.

Again, Gerald May addresses this issue.

> It seems to me that free will is given to us for a purpose:
> so that we may choose freely, without coercion or manipu-
> lation, to love God in return, and to love one another in
> a similarly perfect way. This is the deepest desire of our
> hearts. In other words, our creation is by love, in love, and
> for love. It is both our birthright and our authentic destiny
> to participate fully in this creative loving, and freedom of
> will is essential for our participation to occur.[2]

You and I must be able to make choices freely. Unfortunately, if you have been struggling with crazy-makers in your life, you may be addicted—in a loose sense of the word—to these people. You may be obsessively bound up in trying to change them instead of focusing your heart and soul on loving God, letting Him change you and give you wisdom for better ways of dealing with the situation.

Please understand that it is not simply a case of one or the other, changing the crazy-makers in your life or changing you. Elements of both are at work. The Scriptures encourage us to seek first the kingdom of God and then allow God to work in us to change our situation.

May says that addictions or excessive attachments use up our desire.

> It is like psychic malignancy, sucking our life energy into specific obsessions and compulsions, leaving less and less energy available for people and other pursuits. Spiritually, addiction is a deep-seated form of idolatry. The objects of our addictions become our false gods. These are what we worship, what we attend to, where we give our time and energy, instead of love. Addiction, then, displaces and supplants God's love as the source and object of our deepest true desire.[3]

Our goal, then, is to have some level of detachment from the people and things that cause us to obsess. You know this if you are focused on your struggle with control freaks in your life. The freedom to change you, and perhaps them, comes as you focus on the Lord and allow Him to empower you to make the necessary changes you seek in your life.

If you are excessively attached to a sufferer or aggressor, you know it. Again, the primary goal is to focus on the Lord, allowing Him to empower you to detach so that you are free to make healthier decisions. "Seek first his kingdom and his righteousness, and all these things will be given to you as well" (Matthew 6:33).

The Courage to Change

As I write these words, I am very aware that the crazy-makers in your life may well be people you love or care about. They may have no motive for luring, snaring, hooking, or catching you—but they do. If you didn't care about them, you probably wouldn't struggle with them. You'd have walked away by now. But you do care, and that makes detaching all the more challenging. In such circumstances, in addition to the power of God, change requires one thing—courage.

The word is adapted from the French word *corage* or *curage*, which also connoted the idea that *courage* comes from the heart as the seat of feeling, thought, spirit, mind, disposition, and nature. The root of *courage* also comes from the Latin word for courage, *corāticum.* The root *cor,* meaning heart, parallels the French word for heart, *cœur.*

Courage is usually used in modern language to describe people who have a quality of heart and mind that allows them to face danger in spite of their fear, which is also often referred to as bravery or boldness. You will need courage to do these things in your journey to freedom:

- stand firm when the control freak tries to tell you what to do
- disagree with the borderline who wants to twist your words
- leave when the aggressor threatens to become physically or verbally aggressive
- tell the sufferer you cannot give her any more physical, emotional, or financial help
- inform the egotist you also want time to share your point of view
- make choices every day to honor your feelings, thoughts, and desired goals

The fuel that drives you forward will be courage—heart and passion. You need to feel it down to the tips of your toes if you want to move forward. If you cannot find this passion for freedom, you will likely remain lukewarm, and this will not propel you forward. In fact, it will keep you stuck in situations that quite likely are dangerous to you either emotionally or perhaps even physically.

The Cost to Change

To stay the same is easier in many ways. As the saying goes, "I'd rather deal with the demons I know than the devil I don't." That saying may be more true than we know.

We feel comfortable in sticking with the troubles we have rather than changing and facing completely new trials. Our ruts may be difficult to handle, but at least we are familiar with them.

Remember the scenario from an earlier chapter where the husband struggled with a gambling addiction? I refer to this couple often when discussing the cost of change. When faced with the cost of treatment—that he would have to give up frequenting casinos and she would have to do whatever was necessary to escape his wrath—they decided the price was simply too high. They walked away to resume their old, dysfunctional lives. He would not give up his gambling; she would not face her codependence.

From the outside looking in, the casual observer might wonder, *Why in the world would he not give up his gambling addiction? Why would she not give up her addiction to him in exchange for freedom?* But we know the answer because each of us, in one way or another, knows their struggle. We have our own areas of attachment that we refuse to face or give up. Change is costly.

Consider your attachments for a moment. I'm not talking about the things you enjoy in this life, such as your summer cabin, sailboat, or motor home. I'm talking about the things or people that have you *attached*—derived from the French root word *attacher*—"nailed to." What are you attached to that would be very hard to give up? We are all nailed to someone or something to some degree. We all know the cost of giving this up would be great.

You may think I am being a bit dramatic, comparing the cost of leaving an addiction to the cost of letting go of our habitual way of interacting with a crazy-maker. However, the comparison is fair. Dealing with a crazy-maker can become something of an addiction. The crazy-maker's hooks may be deeply embedded in you, and freeing yourself may be more of a challenge than you think.

Not long ago I conducted some research into why victims of domestic violence struggle to leave abusers (aggressors). At first glance, we all say, "Why do you take it? Just leave him. Get out and teach him a lesson." But again, freedom is not so easily attained. We forget the cost of such dramatic change.

My research uncovered an explanation that may be useful to you as we consider the cost of change. In a phenomenon called *trauma bonding,* the interplay between good times and bad, love and hate, joy and sorrow, creates an incredibly powerful bond. The bond solidi-fies. At times, nothing seems to be able to pry the victim and abuser apart. In fact, any law enforcement officer will tell you that the most dangerous situation in which to intervene is a domestic dispute. In a moment, the victim can turn on the officer. She quickly becomes a sufferer, firmly attached to her accustomed situation.

I recently counseled a 45-year-old woman named Denise. After several years of dating Barry, a control freak, she felt as if she could no longer cope with his controlling tactics. During one of our final individual counseling sessions, she decided to leave him. She offered these words:

"Leaving Barry is not as easy as others might think. Even though I've decided I can't stand to have him micro-managing my life any-more, I'm going to miss his playfulness. No one I've dated is as much fun as he is. I'm going to miss that. For us, the good times are very, very good, and the bad times are very bad. Leaving him means I have to take a chance that there's someone better out there for me, and I'm not sure that's true. This is extremely frightening for me."

She had clearly expressed the essence of trauma bonding: "The good times are very, very good, and the bad times are very bad." The mixture of good times with bad creates a powerful adhesive that is hard to break.

The Scriptures offer a lesson in knowing the cost of any en-deavor.

> Suppose one of you wants to build a tower. Will he not first sit down and estimate the cost to see if he has enough money to complete it? For if he lays the foundation and is not able to finish it, everyone who sees it will ridicule him, saying, "This fellow began to build and was not able to finish" (Luke 14:28-30).

What does this Scripture have to do with you and changing how you interact with the crazy-maker in your life? The Scripture tells us that thorough planning is healthy for any project. Only a fool rushes headlong into something. The tools offered in this book will help you make the difficult changes in your life.

The Consequences of Change

If I have learned one thing about change, it is this: Change does not happen in one fell swoop. It is the result of numerous small steps, many of which you have already begun taking. Change is also not linear. If you look back over your life, you will see the jagged, seesaw path of change. A seed of restlessness led you to become more frustrated and perhaps even angry. Now you are ready to take bigger steps to transform your life.

You have counted the cost of change. Perhaps it includes summoning the courage to leave a control freak or insist that the aggressor go in for anger management. Or perhaps it includes learning to end the triangulation your mother or father have created in your family. Perhaps you have an image of what you'd like to see changed, and now you are considering the consequences of embarking on this journey.

As Denise said to me, the ripples of change reach out a long way. Let's consider some of the consequences of change.

First, changing our circumstances changes us. We cannot predict all the things that will change when we start making modifications in our lives, but one thing is certain—we will change.

After my divorce a number of years ago, a series of additional alterations took place, a veritable cascade of circumstances. I moved to our vacation home, which took me to a new city, where I set up a new counseling practice. Soon I became involved in the local Baptist church, making friends and participating in the Sunday school classes. Now that I was living close to my sailboat, I was able to participate more actively in this passion. I developed a new group of friends and acquaintances. As much as I initially resisted this change, I found that it forced me to grow and deepen as a person.

Second, when we change, those around us often change as well. I have shared how one person can make a world of difference in a family or marriage if she will consider doing things in a new and different way. If you learn to set boundaries on an aggressor, for example, he will be forced to accept positive change or face the reality of living without you. If you tell the egotist in your life that you want to meet for lunch but need to make sure you are able to talk about something important to you, the relationship stands a much better chance of growing.

Third, when we change, we open our lives up to new possibilities. Have you heard the story of the monkey who put his hand in the jar for food, but his fist was too large to remove the food? Refusing to let go of his bounty, the monkey starved, all the while clutching his food.

We are often like the starving monkey. We want it all and refuse to embrace change for fear that we'll starve in some way. Like the monkey, we must be willing to relinquish something in order to get something else. When we release the familiar, we literally create space for wonderful new possibilities to enter our lives.

Fourth, change inevitably creates anxiety. Although adventure is exciting, it is also frightening. If you weren't stretching, you wouldn't feel anxious. If you want to remain safe, stay the same. If you want to grow, stretch a little. Yes, change will cause you to feel some anxiety, but trust God to give you the strength to handle it.

Drs. Cloud and Townsend address this in their book *God Will Make a Way*:

> One of the biggest causes of escalating fear is the "fear of fear"…Everyone has some fear, and that is normal. Make some space for it in your head. Remember, courage is not the absence of fear. Courage is moving forward in the face of fear.[4]

Listen to the words of the psalmist, who certainly faced many dangers as he made courageous decisions:

> Listen to my prayer, O God, do not ignore my plea; hear me and answer me. My thoughts trouble me and I am distraught at the voice of the enemy, at the stares of the wicked; for they bring down suffering upon me and revile me in their anger. My heart is in anguish within me; the terrors of death assail me (Psalm 55:1-4).

Finally, change ultimately brings confidence. After we have made the decision to alter our lives and have embraced the inevitable anxiety, we stretch and grow and become more comfortable with our situation. We gain new skills, new ways of coping, new supportive friends, and a deeper faith.

When Choosing to Leave

Although I believe in doing whatever we can to save marriages and relationships, I am also a realist. The craziness is sometimes simply too much to endure. Some marriages and relationships are so fraught with turmoil and abuse that their sanctity is terminally marred.

What are some of the signs that it may be time to leave? Let me offer a few for your consideration.

- You have endured ongoing verbal or physical violence.
- Your children are in emotional or physical danger.
- You are emotionally and spiritually bereft, unable to sustain the effort to work on the relationship.
- You sense an ongoing erosion of your identity in this crazy-making relationship.
- Sustained and significant acrimony permeates the relationship, and staying seems to only perpetuate this incredible tension.

I offer these as simply guidelines. The decision to leave is highly personal and should only be made when you sense God's peace.

You may choose to leave rather than continue to endure dealing with the crazy-maker. What can be said to help you?

First, know that God has not abandoned you. God knows what He is doing, while we, at times, may not. You have prayed that the heart of someone dear to you would change, but perhaps that has not happened. This doesn't mean God is deaf. It means God is working in ways you might not understand at this time.

Second, God knows what you are experiencing, and He cares. Yes, the God who has numbered the hairs on your head knows the details of your life. The psalmist says, "O LORD, you have searched me and know me. You know when I sit and when I rise; you perceive my thoughts from afar. You discern my going out and my lying down; you are familiar with all my ways" (Psalms 39:1-3).

When I am in the middle of a crisis, I feel small. Knowing that God is bigger than any of my ordeals helps me. He knows what will happen, and everything I experience passes through His sovereign hands.

Third, we all have a free will. The crazy-makers in your life have free will and are responsible for their own actions. Meanwhile, the only person you can control is you. The only person you are responsible for is you. This is important to remember. You can choose to stay for today, or you can choose to leave.

Fourth, leaving may provide the impetus for greater change. Leaving is sometimes the force for change in the crazy-maker. We never know what hitting bottom will be, but for many, a spouse leaving is a major wake-up call. Consider a temporary separation as a line in the sand to which the crazy-maker may respond.

Fifth, don't leave as a manipulative ploy. Be prepared for drastic changes if you choose to leave. The crazy-makers may choose to go on with their lives just as they were before they met you. Some crazy-makers may dive further into their destructive tendencies—and that is their choice.

Finally, know that you can and will be strengthened and changed in this process. The apostle James tells us that trials come to make us stronger. I have talked to many people who have gone through intense struggles with crazy-makers and have been forced to their knees in the process. This can be a very rich time spiritually. Let God do His work in you.

When Choosing to Stay

For some people, leaving is out of the question. You will remain in a relationship with that crazy-maker, perhaps because you are in a marriage and don't want to consider ending it, or perhaps because the crazy-maker is a parent, and you would rather hold on to the good that is in the relationship than give it up entirely. People choose to stay in relationships for many reasons. If you are one of them, what might be helpful for you to hear?

Some of the greatest lessons are found in difficulties. Since you are choosing to stay, and presuming that you sense God wants you to stay, some important lessons are available to you.

The apostle Paul certainly was acquainted with crazy-makers. He was subjected routinely to people who wanted to cause him harm. In the midst of those struggles, he offered this encouragement:

> No temptation has seized you except what is common to man. And God is faithful; he will not let you be tempted beyond what you can bear. But when you are tempted, he will also provide a way out so that you can stand up under it (1 Corinthians 10:13).

Paul wrote those words while he was being treated horrifically. He was repeatedly thrown in prison, shipwrecked, scoffed at, and scorned. He had a "thorn in the flesh" that he asked the Lord to remove but that was never taken away. Amid these struggles he counsels us to "give thanks in all circumstances" (1 Thessalonians 5:18).

I am reminded of the great analyst Viktor Frankl, who suffered in Nazi concentration camps. In his book *Man's Search for Meaning,* Frankl described the moment at which many prisoners learned to be helpless. At one camp, a guard turned to the prisoners as they entered and told them they would never leave. According to Frankl, those who bought into this way of thinking soon died. Those who rejected the guard's ominous prediction and retained a belief that "this too shall pass" had a much higher rate of survival. Frankl had a strong belief that suffering ceases to be suffering when we find meaning in the experience.

Meaning is available to you in your current experience. Rather than feeling like a victim, choose instead to learn as much from the experience as possible.

The Commitment to Change

I hope by now you have an inkling of your direction. Have you been able to identify an aggressor you need to confront or an egotist who needs a dose of humility? Perhaps you have a sufferer friend who has perfected the art of being a victim, and you are dying to set healthier boundaries for yourself.

The key is being committed to the process. You need to have clarity about your goal and the determination to follow through with it.

At this writing, I am in my tenth week of piano lessons. As a fifty-something, trying to get my fingers to do all this strange stuff is no easy matter. I started out strong, practicing half an hour a day, just as my teacher told me. But then came a media tour, a speaking engagement, and a vacation. Suddenly, my enthusiasm waned, and I felt like a victim of the best-laid-plans scenario.

You are probably wired a bit like me—long on good intentions, a bit shorter on follow-through. If so, I can offer a few tips that are helpful to me.

One, keep your eye on the prize. Remember why you are practicing the tools offered in this book. Be careful about slipping back into mindless reactions. Be like the apostle Paul, who said "I press on to take hold of that for which Christ Jesus took hold of me" (Philippians 3:12).

Two, keep your goal simple and practical. You will do better if your objective is measurable and clear. You can keep some practical steps written on your refrigerator:

- Don't let Mom hook me into talking about my brother.
- Don't get angry when Jim starts escalating with me.
- Tell Joan I'm not going to argue with her about our daughters.

You gain power when you choose how you want to respond and then follow through.

Three, feel the joy that comes from following your mission. Meaning and delight can come from pursuing our goals and passions. If setting healthier boundaries is a new passion for you, remember to celebrate each one you set.

Fourth, don't measure progress by the way others react. Measure progress by how well you do at following through with your goals. If you are able to be assertive with a friend, celebrate your ability to take this step, regardless of how the friend responds. Be true to your core values.

Finally, remain mindful. In much of my work with people I ask them to keep a journal—an effort I propose to encourage mindfulness. I want them to be aware, conscious. Too often, I'm reactive, and I want to be less reactive and more active. I want to make better choices and can only do so if I am aware of the choices I currently make and their consequences. Notice the way you act with the crazy-makers in your life. Notice what works and what doesn't. Even this simple exercise offers a hint of detachment and will bring some measure of peace.

Jesus is our ultimate example of being committed to change in spite of the circumstances. He came to earth with a singular mission and followed it completely. He came to earth to bring hope and salvation to a lost people—and doing so would require change from us. He chose a path of humility, and our attitude should mirror His.

> Your attitude should be the same as that of Christ Jesus: Who, being in very nature God, did not consider equality with God something to be grasped, but made himself nothing, taking the very nature of a servant, being made in human likeness. And being found in appearance as a man, he humbled himself and became obedient to death—even death on a cross (Philippians 2:5-8).

Finding Safety

You have difficult decisions to make. Perhaps you will choose to stay involved with the crazy-maker in your life, in which case you'll need all the tools discussed in this book in order to maintain your personal health and well-being. Perhaps you will decide to stay but practice detachment, or perhaps it is time to leave because the chaos is simply too much to endure. Whatever your decision, know that safety is available to you.

The Scriptures are clear—you are safe in the cleft of the rock that is God. The psalmist uses the imagery of protection in the rock 24 times. "The LORD is my rock, my fortress and my deliverer; my God is my rock, in whom I take refuge. He is my shield and the horn of my salvation, my stronghold" (Psalm 18:2).

These are not just words to make us feel better. Protection from the hooks of the crazy-maker is a spiritual reality. Does that mean we will always be delivered from their onslaught? No. It means we will find peace that passes understanding. Even when dealing with crazy-makers, we can know peace. We attain that peace in one way—finding protection in the Rock.

God bless you in the days ahead as you embark on changes that are sure to improve your life. I say with the apostle Paul, "He who began a good work in you will carry it on to completion until the day of Christ Jesus" (Philippians 1:6).

Notes

Chapter 2—Broken Chaos Detectors

1. Christina Baldwin, *Life's Companion* (New York: Bantam Books, 1991), 75.
2. Ibid.
3. Harriet Lerner, *The Dance of Deception* (New York: HarperCollins Publishers, 1993), 26.
4. Ibid.
5. Ibid., 88.

Chapter 3—They Come in All Kinds

1. Gary Chapman, *Loving Solutions* (Chicago: Northfield Publishing, 1998), 197.
2. Christine Ann Lawson, *Understanding the Borderline Mother* (Northvale, NJ: Jason Aronson, 2000), 80.
3. Paul Meier, *Don't Let the Jerks Get the Best of You* (Nashville: Thomas Nelson, 1993), 35.

Chapter 4—Control Freaks

1. Paul Meier and Robert Wise, *Crazy Makers* (Nashville: Thomas Nelson, 2003), 9.
2. Ibid., 32.
3. Patricia Evans, *Controlling People* (Avon, MA: Adams Media Corporation, 2002), 184.
4. Gary Chapman, *Loving Solutions* (Chicago: Northfield Publishing, 1998), 102.

Chapter 5—The Big Hook: Aggressors and Egotists

1. Albert Bernstein, *Emotional Vampires* (New York: McGraw Hill, 2001), 69.
2. Ibid., 71.
3. Ibid., 74.

4. Ibid., 132.
5. Patricia Evans, *Controlling People* (Avon, MA: Adams Media Corporation, 2002), 54.

Chapter 6—The Big Hook: Borderlines, Sufferers, and Control Freaks

1. Marsha Linehan, *Cognitive Behavioral Treatment of Borderline Personality Disorder* (New York: Guilliford Press, 1993).
2. Gary Chapman, *Loving Solutions* (Chicago: Northfield Publishing, 1998), 136.
3. Randi Kreger, *Stop Walking on Eggshells* (Oakland: New Harbinger Publications, 2002), 84.
4. Chapman, 137.
5. Patricia Evans, *Controlling People* (Avon, MA: Adams Media Corporation, 2002), 254.

Chapter 7—The Net of Deception

1. Scott Peck, *The Road Less Traveled* (New York: Simon & Schuster, 1978), 62.
2. Ibid., 63.
3. Robert Bramson, *Coping with Difficult People* (New York: Ballantine Books, 1981), 96.
4. Ibid., 135.
5. Les Parrott, *The Control Freak* (Wheaton: Tyndale House Publishers, 2000), 34.
6. John Bradshaw, *Healing the Shame That Binds You* (Deerfield Beach, FL: Health Communications, 1988).
7. Albert Bernstein, *Emotional Vampires* (New York: McGraw Hill, 2001), 80.
8. Harriet Lerner, *The Dance of Deception* (New York: HarperCollins Publishers, 1993), 36.

Chapter 8—Foul Bait and Other Crazy-Making Lures

1. Randi Kreger, *Stop Walking on Eggshells* (Oakland: New Harbinger Publications, 2002), 57.

Chapter 9—The Powerful Bait of Irresponsibility

1. Scott Peck, *The Road Less Traveled* (New York: Simon & Schuster, 1978), 36.
2. Ibid.
3. Gerald May, *Addiction and Grace* (San Francisco: HarperSanFrancisco, 1988), 176.
4. John Gottman, *Why Marriages Succeed or Fail* (New York: Simon & Schuster, 1994), 79.
5. Albert Bernstein, *Emotional Vampires* (New York: McGraw-Hill, 2001), 19.
6. Sam Keen, *To Love and Be Loved* (New York: Bantam Books, 1997), 118.
7. Ibid., 114.

8. Ibid., 119.
9. Gary Chapman, *Loving Solutions* (Chicago: Northfield Publishing, 1998), 85.
10. Harriet Lerner, *The Dance of Anger* (New York: HarperPerennial, 1985), 138-39.

Chapter 10—Boundaries Deliver Freedom

1. John Bradshaw, *Homecoming* (New York: Bantam Books, 1990), 8.
2. Robert Hemfelt, Frank Minirth, and Paul Meier, *Love Is a Choice* (Nashville: Thomas Nelson Publishers, 1989), 28.
3. Michael Gurian, *Love's Journey* (Boston: Shambhala Publications, 1995), 106.
4. Henry Cloud and John Townsend, *Boundaries* (Grand Rapids: Zondervan, 1992), 24.
5. Ibid., 26.
6. Ibid., 104-5.
7. Henri Nouwen, *Here and Now* (New York: Crossroads, 1994), 131.
8. Charles Whitfield, *Boundaries and Relationships* (Deerfield Beach, FL: Health Communications, Inc., 1993), 17-38.

Chapter 11—The Freedom of Normalcy

1. Albert Bernstein, *Emotional Vampires* (New York: McGraw Hill, 2001), 14.
2. Anne Lamott, *Traveling Mercies* (New York: Pantheon Books, 1999), 248.
3. Nora Roberts, *Blue Dahlia* (New York: Jove Books, 2004), 117.
4. Patricia Evans, *Controlling People* (Avon, MA: Adams Media Corporation, 2002), 40.
5. John Bradshaw, *Homecoming* (New York: Bantam Books, 1990), 192-93.
6. Julia Cameron, *The Artist's Way* (New York: Jeremy P. Tarcher, 1992), 44.
7. Ibid., 53.

Chapter 12—Total Freedom: Catch and Release

1. Gerald May, *Addiction and Grace* (San Francisco: HarperSanFrancisco: 1988), 2.
2. Ibid., 13.
3. Ibid.
4. Henry Cloud and John Townsend, *God Will Make a Way* (Nashville: Integrity Publishers, 2002), 198.

Dr. Hawkins is interested in hearing
about your journey and may be
contacted through his website at
www.YourRelationshipDoctor.com